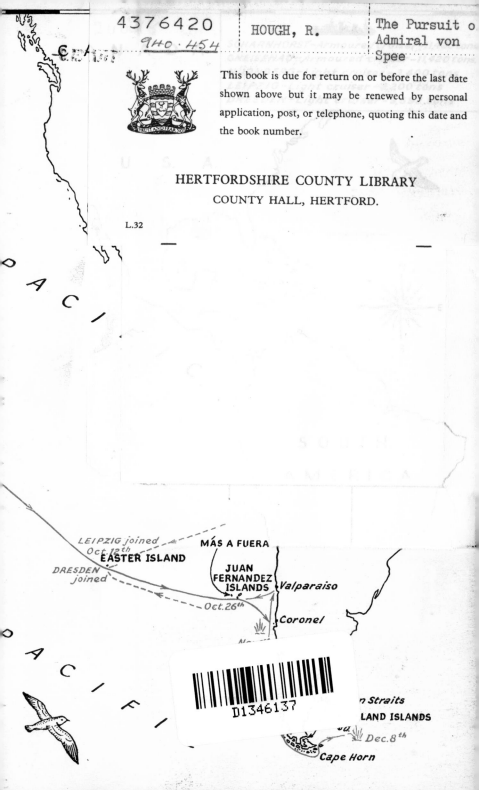

PACI

LEIPZIG joined
Oct.12th
DRESDEN
joined

EASTER ISLAND

MÁS A FUERA

JUAN
FERNANDEZ
ISLANDS

Valparaiso

Oct.26th

Coronel

PACIFI

n Straits
LAND ISLANDS

Dec.8th
Cape Horn

The Pursuit of Admiral von Spee

The Pursuit of
Admiral von Spee

RICHARD HOUGH

London
GEORGE ALLEN AND UNWIN LTD
RUSKIN HOUSE MUSEUM STREET

FIRST PUBLISHED IN 1969

This book is copyright under the Berne Convention. Apart from any
fair dealing for the purpose of private study, research, criticism or
review, as permitted under the Copyright Act, 1956, no portion
may be reproduced by any process without written permission.
Enquiries should be addressed to the publishers.

© *Richard Hough*, 1969
SBN 04 943013 0

PRINTED IN GREAT BRITAIN
in 11 on 12 pt Ehrhardt
AT THE SHENVAL PRESS
LONDON, HERTFORD AND HARLOW

FOR JULIET

Acknowledgements

My special thanks are due to Rear-Admiral H. E. Dannreuter, DSO, RN, and Captain W. R. C. Steele, RN, who served together in HMS *Invincible* at the Battle of the Falkland Islands; to Commander W. B. Rowbotham, RN, and Lieutenant-Commander P. K. Kemp, OBE, RN, of the Historical Department of the Ministry of Defence, Navy; Rear-Admiral E. M. Eller, USN, Director of Naval History, US Navy Department; Miss Jennie Yamashita and Miss Agnes C. Conrad of the Hawaii State Library; and Mrs Renate Matthews and Herr Rainer Tamchina for providing translations from German sources and checking the manuscript.

Acknowledgments are due to the following authors and publishers for permission to quote copyright material: Messrs Charles Scribner's Sons, and the Hamlyn Publishing Group Ltd (*The World Crisis* by Winston Churchill), Barrie Pitt, Esq (*Coronel and Falkland*); Her Majesty's Stationery Office (*Naval Operations* by Sir Julian Corbett); Messrs Jonathan Cape Ltd (*Fear God and Dread Nought: the Correspondence of Admiral of the Fleet Lord Fisher of Kilverstone* edited by Arthur J. Marder); Messrs William Kimber and Co Ltd (*Sailor at Sea* by Harold Hickling); Hutchinson Publishing Group Ltd (*Before Jutland: Admiral von Spee's Last Voyage* by Hans Pochhammer, and *Command of the Far Seas* by Keith Middlemass); Messrs Peter Davies Ltd (*Coronel and After* by Lloyd Hirst).

Most of the contents of this
book appeared originally
in *The New Yorker*, in
slightly different form

Preface

The two historic naval actions at Coronel and the Falkland Islands mark the culminating points of one of the greatest sea hunts of modern times. I am concerned in this book mainly with the German side of the events, and the experiences and conduct of the German commander-in-chief. He was Vice-Admiral Maximilian von Spee, a brave and resourceful officer who sailed his supremely efficient but isolated squadron right across the Pacific Ocean, pursued by the fighting ships of Britain, Japan, France, Australia and New Zealand. The chase and the deadly clashes of arms which first interrupted and finally terminated it, have for long fascinated me. As a boy, the judgements of fate off the dark Chilean coast in November, and then on that shining December morning thirty-six days later on the brink of the Antarctic; the fateful inevitability of total failure or total defeat which hung over the thousands of men (and boys too) who were swept into such impersonal and annihilating combat in remote seas; the fearful manner of their death—all these features of the pursuit of Admiral von Spee haunted my imagination and filled me with wonder. Only later did I learn of the more oblique and tragicomic overtones, and they tempted me to recount the story in detail.

This, then, is a brief and informal account of the curious, the valorous, and the fearful events in the life of Admiral von Spee, and the men who sailed with him, pursued him and fought him, from August 4 to December 8, 1914.

Richard Hough   January 1968

Contents

Illustrations

CHAPTER 1

Von Spee: Naval Colonist

Within a few weeks of the opening of the First World War in 1914, and while the German armies fought their way triumphantly through Belgium and France and almost to Paris itself, most of Germany's new colonial empire was lost for ever to its owners. Only certain areas of German Africa held out. The rest of the numerous colonies, from Togoland to the Bismarck Archipelago in the Pacific, were captured by the soldiers of Britain, France, Japan, South Africa, Australia and New Zealand. The rapid victory of the Japanese at Tsingtau, for example, or the assault on Samoa by a party of New Zealanders and the British bombardment of Dar-es-Salaam, were all made possible because the British navy, supported by the fighting ships of her allies, controlled the oceans of the world. Even in European waters, where the Germans possessed an unhappily named High Seas Fleet only slightly less numerous than the British Grand Fleet, the most powerful in the world, Britannia ruled the waves. (The German officers and men were lusting for combat, but cautious strategical considerations demanded that they must remain only as a threat, a 'fleet in being': there was to be no fighting yet.) The British Expeditionary Force was transported safely across the Channel to France. British and French trade continued almost uninterrupted, while German merchantmen all over the world sought refuge in neutral waters and harbours.

This neat pattern of omnipotence at sea shown on the Admiralty's War Room map was spoiled by a scattering of hostile emblems. Each of these signified a German cruiser. On the north China coast, at Germany's rich colonial port of Tsingtau, there was a heavier concentration of enemy markings. All these cruisers were fast and of modern design. Their ancestors were the American and French corsairs which had plagued British trade during the wars of the eighteenth and nineteenth centuries. Without exception, the commanders of these German cruisers were officers of the highest calibre. They had been selected by Grand Admiral Alfred von

Tirpitz (the creator of the new German navy) for their ability in peacetime 'to show the German flag' both to their rival imperialists and to their own colonial natives in appropriate style, to counter with firmness any uprisings, and generally to bring credit to the Fatherland wherever they might sail. When war came, this élite band of captains were trained to adapt themselves to the new circumstances, to be skilful in evasion, resolute in combat, and fully prepared, in the words of one of them, 'to sell our lives dearly'. Their ships were too few to delay seriously the destruction of the German Empire. Their enterprise was the dangerous one of the *guerre de course*. Soon they were deprived of their bases to rest and refit their ships and to replenish their ammunition, and they had to live on their wits and what they could find, like any Elizabethan or Barbary pirate. But unlike their forebears, they were handicapped by the need to conform to the new international laws intended to humanize the conduct of war at sea against unarmed merchantmen, and the elaborate regulations which restricted their use of neutral waters and harbours.

All these German cruiser commanders matched up to the high ideals established by their Grand Admiral and acquitted themselves chivalrously and magnificently before, one by one, they were hunted down by a superior enemy. They extracted a high price before succumbing. Captain Karl von Müller of the *Emden* sank seventeen merchantmen in the Indian Ocean. Operating off the eastern United States seaboard and in Caribbean and South American waters, Captain Köhler for a brief time wrought havoc among the Atlantic shipping lanes and sank 68,000 tons of British cargo ships with his cruiser *Karlsruhe*. Captain Lüdecke of the *Dresden* survived the longest, and at one time attracted a hunting force of some thirty men-of-war before his cruiser was sunk off the coast of Chile. Another cruiser captain sank a warship and many merchantmen and hazarded troop convoys and communications in the Red Sea and Indian Ocean. All these hostile and damaging activities resulted in as much distress to the British as John Paul Jones and his fellow American Captain Isaac Hull had caused more than one hundred years earlier. It was an affront to a nation which had put so much trust and so much money into its navy to read accounts of its merchantmen being halted in mid-ocean, their crews taken off (and well provided for: the war at sea was to remain a gentlemen's business until the submarines later got down to their ugly work in earnest), and then sunk. Not until every one of these raiding cruisers had gone to the bottom was full British confidence in her navy regained.

Because of his skill and his power, of the legends which built up about him as well as the dangers and mysteries of his movements about the oceans of the world, the man most feared by the British was Admiral Count von Spee. Von Spee, a stern, religious and dedicated warrior-aristocrat, with interests in natural history and the intricacies of auction bridge, was the most successful German cruiser commander of them all. With his squadron based on Tsingtau, but soon to be cast homeless on the great expanse of the Pacific Ocean, von Spee took the leading role in a series of events ranging from the trivial and comic to the most magnificent levels of heroism and triumph and tragedy between August 4 and December 8, 1914.

Maximilian Johannes Maria Hubertus Reichsgraf von Spee had been a child of the new German nation and its boundless imperial and military ambitions. He was a boy of five when Bismarck led Prussia triumphantly against Austria, a youth at the time of the Franco-Prussian War and the proclamation of Wilhelm I as Emperor of Germany. While the vitality of the country was finding expression in new industrial and commercial activities that brought forth wonder and then increasing anxiety from the older powers of Europe, Maximilian was passing through adolescence to young manhood. The Spee family was one of the oldest and most respected in Prussia, and Maximilian could trace his ancestry back as far as 1166. There had been a Friedrich Spe in the sixteenth century who was a noted poet and Jesuit and had taken a leading part in efforts to stamp out witchcraft. The family had been ennobled by Charles VI in the early part of the eighteenth century. Maximilian's father, Reichsgraf Rudolf, had married a Danish woman, Fernande Tutein, and Maximilian had been born in Copenhagen on June 22, 1861, the last of five sons. He was brought up as a strict Catholic and was educated privately at the family castle at Heltorf in the Rhine province, at their house at Lucerne in Switzerland, and at the *Gymnasium*. At the age of sixteen he entered the Imperial German Navy as a cadet. From the time he passed out as a sub-lieutenant, von Spee's professional career became increasingly identified with the rise in power of his service and the colonial expansion of his country. He was destined to take a leading part in the seizure of

Germany's first colonies. He was to witness the spectacular rise in imperial power of his country in some twenty-five years, and then—at close hand—the downfall of the greater part of this empire within a few weeks. As he rose in rank from cadet to admiral, the power of the Imperial German Navy was increased a hundredfold from a heterogeneous collection of gunboats and coast defence vessels to the second most powerful fighting fleet in the world. When war at last broke out against the first imperial power, von Spee was to lead his squadron in two of Germany's most decisive naval actions.

In April 1884, Maximilian von Spee was a fine, well set-up full lieutenant, tall and broad-shouldered and straight-backed 'as if he had swallowed a broom handle'. He had a fair complexion, fair wavy hair and deep-set blue eyes. His contemporaries described him as devout in his religious faith, serious and studious, and a rigid disciplinarian. He was already clearly destined for high office in his career. It was at this time, while he was still only twenty-two years of age, that he was given the opportunity to demonstrate his initiative and physical endurance as an officer-colonist.

In the late 1870s and early 1880s Chancellor Bismarck had become increasingly conscious of the need for his country to match the colonial activities of Britain and France and other nations in Africa, the Far East and the Pacific. Many great German commercial houses had set up trading posts in these areas, and their business was being increasingly jeopardized by the more aggressive methods of the old colonial powers, who would under force of arms persuade local chieftains to sign exclusive protection and trading treaties, or would even annexe, say, a few dozen islands in the Pacific or a few thousand square miles of African territory. Bismarck had the support and encouragement of the German commercial houses like Godeffroy of Hamburg and Hernshein (Samoan copra) and Lüderitz of Bremen, and of many scientists and explorers, whose 'Central Society for Commercial Geography and German Interests Abroad' became increasingly influential. But he had to tread carefully because of political opposition at home and increasing French and British suspicion of his motives. For a number of years he held back from taking any active steps. When he decided to move, he moved swiftly, in order to present the opponents at home and abroad with a *fait accompli*. The man he chose to set up Germany's African colonial empire was a doctor of medicine and a valiant and experienced explorer, Gustav Nachtigal. Dr Nachtigal was fifty years old, a tubby little man with dark hair, blue eyes and a weatherbeaten face. He is described as 'gay with his friends, reserved with strangers'. At the time of his commission 'to place certain coastal areas of West Africa under German protection', he was consul-general in Tunisia. His explorations in Africa and Asia had left him physically vulnerable, and he had come to this part of North Africa (where he was also physician to the Bey of Tunis) for the sake of his lungs. He knew that the West African climate was the worst possible for his health, and accepted his orders with reluctance. After begging permission to be allowed to bring his old friend and fellow-explorer Dr Max Buchner with him, he sailed for Marseilles and thence travelled overland to Lisbon to meet the ship that was to take him on his first and last colonizing mission.

SMS *Möwe* was a gun vessel of only 848 tons. Quarters were cramped for the commander and six officers, and most of the internal space unoccupied by ammunition for the 15-centimetre and 12-centimetre guns and rifles was filled with gifts for the natives; for this was, if possible, to be an errand of friendly persuasion rather than of physical violence. Among the officers who had been selected for the delicate and even dangerous mission of establishing a German empire in Africa was Lieutenant Maximilian Count von Spee. He was gratified by the honour bestowed on him. On the night before sailing from Germany's principal naval base at Kiel on April 15th there had been a small celebratory party at the casino. On such an occasion von Spee was prepared to relax with a cigar and a *krug* of beer. His elder brother Ferdinand—later to become a privy councillor at Kiel—was present, and had brought with him a quantity 'of small knick-knacks to trade to the negroes', as Maximilian wrote home to his mother a few days later, 'which I hope I shall be able to do as such things are very rarely brought to those parts'.

The real purpose of the expedition had not been publicly announced; instead, Bismarck let it be known to the English Government that Dr Nachtigal would 'proceed shortly to the West Coast of Africa to report on the measures which may be necessary to protect German interests in those regions'. The naval officers at Kiel knew better, and as von Spee recorded, 'we left ... accompanied by cheers from the boats and our colleagues on shore; the whole thing made a splendid impression'. Britain and the other African colonial powers remained suspicious of the *Möwe* and those aboard her. When Dr Nachtigal joined the vessel in the Tagus at Lisbon on May 10th, speculation further increased. The reception in Portugal, one of Europe's oldest colonial nations and with a heavy stake in Africa, was not cordial. In the course of an audience with King Luiz at Necessidades Palace, Dr Nachtigal was asked about the real purpose of the journey, but to the vexation of the King the doctor evaded the question. Von Spee described this incident in a typically informative letter home. The Portuguese 'are very suspicious', he reported. 'Portugal is too weak to found new colonies; on the other hand, she resents it when others search for them in countries whose discovery they claim and where they believe they have the first right.'

The little *Möwe* left Lisbon with no regrets among the officers, who had also found the city an expensive place, and proceeded down the coast of Portugal to Gibraltar and across to the Moroccan coast. By mid-June the gunboat had reached the rich and humid shores of Senegal, a coastline which was already the scene of energetic British and French activity. Doctors Nachtigal and Buchner, supported by armed parties led by von Spee and the other officers, proceeded ashore on the Los Islands and explored up the estuary of the Debreka. They made contact with local chieftains, who appeared to be curiously familiar with the various wordings and forms of treaties of friendship, protection and annexation which Dr Nachtigal produced and indicated that they should sign. For colonists, this was evidently not virgin soil. However, contracts were signed (with a mark by the chieftains) and exchanged and the German flag hoisted on masts hastily erected in suitably prominent situations. In spite of the speed and decisiveness of the operations, von Spee nursed doubts that they had so far accomplished very much. 'It is of course a secret,' he wrote, 'but I don't think we shall finally succeed because there are already treaties with the French and the British in existence.'

They sailed on south and east along the African coast, their zeal undiminished, calling at the remote trading posts of great German commercial houses like Thormählen, Woermann and Jantzen, reassuring the anxious officials by their presence and their evident determination to put the territory under the German flag. During the following few weeks the West African coastline was subjected to the close attention of French, German and British gunboats, all intent on acquiring strips of land, from a few acres to hundreds of square miles, by means that varied from friendly persuasion, through bribery and threats, to naked armed force. Wherever these annexation parties travelled, they met evidence of the activities of their competitors. On several occasions, the men-of-war sighted one another. Once the *Möwe* was followed by a French gunboat. 'It is assumed that it wanted to find out who we were and what we were doing,' wrote von Spee. 'We therefore left ostensibly in the direction of Lagos . . . but changed course during the night.' Little Popo was the scene of especially keen competition. Here the *Möwe* received reinforcements in the shape of the 2,169 ton corvette *Sophie*, which was loaded with native hostages. Dr Nachtigal called together a meeting of local kings, and when they had all signed their lands away to the protection of Kaiser Wilhelm, the hostages were released. Von Spee was evidently moved by what followed. 'The welcome by their relatives was very warm and there was great jubilation when they were told they would be freed.' Unhappily one of the kings failed to sign at the last moment, so they were all recaptured and returned into custody. Von Spee also learnt that the King of Togo had been promised £1,600 by the English if he drove off the German colonists. Dr Nachtigal, in his turn, promised his monarch's full protection if they would not sign any more treaties with the opposition. Everyone gladly agreed to this, even the king who had earlier shown reluctance, so the hostages went home after all.

The German party were less successful at gathering together the local tribal leaders farther along the coast. 'All the chiefs have left for Abome,' von Spee recorded, 'where the king, or sultan, is giving a feast which is supposed to consist mainly of killing people.' At Batanga, they were more accessible. 'King Toko came on board and everybody liked his appearance,' von Spee wrote to his mother. 'He wore bright red trousers and coat and an old naval officer's hat. On a long chain round his neck he wore a heart-shaped silver plaque with his name and the name of the donor inscribed on it. One of his companions wore a red tail-coat and instead of trousers only a sort of apron, with a light grey top hat.' Then as the German flag was hoisted over this new German colony for the first time 'one man appeared naked carrying only a sunshade and an admiral's tricorne hat'.

As Dr Nachtigal, von Spee and their armed parties mopped up Kamerun, the territory between the Niger Delta and Gabon, and a number of other areas, a shrewd and ambitious German merchant from Bremen, one F. A. E. Lüderitz, was working up from the south. The valuable and temperate port of Angra Pequena was the first to fall. 'In executing this supreme command,' ran the proclamation of August 10th, 'I here hoist as external sign the Imperial German Flag, and hereby place the . . . territory under the protection and sovereignty of His Majesty the Emperor Wilhelm the First, and call upon you to join me in three cheers for His Majesty . . .' It was a sound that was heard frequently during July and August of 1884. After this Lüderitz sent an agent inland to parley with a Hottentot chief who gave up 150 square miles of territory for 200 rifles, 2,000 marks 'and an assortment of toys, mostly lead soldiers'. From this start there rapidly developed the vast and abundantly rich colony of German West Africa.

The British and French were making some equally useful conquests, too, but they had been surprised by the speed of the German operations and were put out by their success. At the same time they attempted to diminish their importance. *The Times*, reflecting the half-anxious, half-patronizing view of Lord Derby's ministry and the greatest imperial power in the world, hoped that Germany would now be satisfied. The German press, *The Times* reminded its readers, had 'for some time been crying out for a colony of some kind, as a child weeps for want of a toy; and now that a toy colony had been given to it . . . we may expect to have fewer manifestations here of ill humour towards England'. In fact by the time von Spee returned home a year after his departure, Germany's empire in Africa had been consolidated. The numerous protectorates established by the *Möwe* in West Africa had been enlarged, Togoland and Kamerun were safely German, and a vast area in East Africa, too, had been quietly annexed. Unhappily, among those who had taken a leading part in this empire-building, there had been numerous casualties, caused by accidents and by the unhealthy climate. Dr Nachtigal died, as he had expected, of a fever on board the *Möwe* on April 20, 1885, his mission fulfilled. Lüderitz 'disappeared both figuratively and literally from the scene (in South West Africa), for he fell into the Orange River and drowned'. Von Spee himself suffered such a severe attack of rheumatic fever that his constitution was weakened for the rest of his life.

The rise in Maximilian von Spee's fortunes continued to be linked with the spreading power of the new German empire. There was an ever-increasing demand for officials of all kinds to run these colonies (which were soon to cover an area a hundred times greater than Germany itself); and it was in the administrative role of Port Commander of Kamerun that von Spee returned to the dark continent in 1887. There were links with the past to remind him daily of that earlier pioneering voyage which had yielded such rich results. The official steamer which he used to go about his duties was named the *Nachtigal* after the late explorer-colonist, and as cabin boy and personal servant he employed a young native, the son of one of the dispossessed kings. Before von Spee had left home he had become engaged to a young Baroness, Margarete, the daughter of Baron von der Osten Sacken of the house of Wangen in Kurland. During his period of office in Kamerun, he addressed many letters home to her, always of a most informative and earnest nature. He wrote to her in detail about his work, about the unsatisfactory nature of many things and how they were going to be put right, in philosophical admiration of the natural beauties of the country, in grave wonder at the more curious aspects of life. 'Here is a white woman who was mad enough to marry a negro, the missionary,' he once wrote to Margarete. 'I suppose it takes all sorts to make a world.'

Renewed attacks of rheumatic fever obliged von Spee to return to Germany. After his recovery he married Margarete in 1889. They had two sons, Otto and Heinrich, who were to join their father in the service he loved, and were to fight alongside him in their young manhood; and a daughter, Huberta. This was a happy period for von Spee. He was serving in home waters, in the training ship *Moltke*, where he demonstrated his talent for attracting the loyalty of those who served under him. 'He was in charge of a division of boys who were devoted to him,' wrote one of his contemporaries, 'just as he was respected by all his other subordinates. He was also a favourite in the wardroom. He made everybody his friend by his invariable kindness, his unaffected and engaging nature and his dry sense of humour. I sat next to him for eighteen months and during that time I got to know him and appreciate him more every day . . . I believe I can say without exaggeration that none of us ever found even the smallest fault with Count Spee.'

There is no recorded hint of criticism of von Spee either as an officer or family man. His service career appears to be a model of its kind with regular promotion and ever-increasing responsibilities. His admirable record and his rank as a nobleman brought him privileged commissions and the opportunity to play a further part in the extension of Germany's colonial empire, this time in the Far East. In 1897 he was appointed flag-lieutenant of the 7,300-ton first class cruiser *Deutschland* which was to carry His Royal Highness Prince Heinrich of Prussia on a mission to provide both a show of royal grandeur and threatening imperial power to parts of Germany's troubled eastern empire.

Much of this empire had been acquired in the same year of 1884, and with the same relentless speed and efficiency, as the African empire. Merchant pioneers like Godeffroy and Son in Samoa and the Jaluit Company in the Marshall Islands had for many years been successfully trading in the Pacific, and by agreements with native chieftains had acquired exclusive rights in the rich local products— from copra and ivory and pearls to coffee, tobacco and phosphates. When these scattered but immensely rich German trading out-posts found themselves—like their counterparts in West Africa— threatened by the more aggressive imperialism of the French and British, who backed their treaties with native rulers with force and territorial acquisition, Germany took immediate counter steps. Bismarck had issued a 'White Book' (an official government publica-tion) entitled *German Interests in the South Seas* which stressed the importance of 'Germany considering how she can secure for her trade the larger and as yet unexhausted portion of the South Sea Islands'. He also anticipated this report by despatching to the east another explorer-colonist, one Dr Finsch. 'With two warships in the background,' as one historian described the expedition, 'Dr Finsch and his associates sailed about the coasts of New Guinea and New Britain, leaving a trail of German flags behind them until their supply was exhausted.' New names appeared on the map. The northern part of New Guinea became Kaiser Wilhelmsland, New Britain New Pommern, the Duke of York Islands New Lauenberg, New Ireland New Mecklenburg—all to the wrath of the English, who had only recently renamed and 'acquired' them for themselves. Countless numbers of larger and smaller islands fell under German 'protection', including most of the Solomon Islands and a vast collection north of New Guinea, which were honoured with the collective title the Bismarck Archipelago.

Germany was slower off the mark in China. In the mid-1890s France, Britain, Russia and Japan were all jostling one another for concessions and exclusive spheres of influence (the euphemisms were numerous and ingenious) on the Chinese coast. Japan had even gone to war with China in 1895 but had not done very well out of it because the other major powers had curtailed her territorial ambitions by the Treaty of Shimonoseki. Germany had obtained two modest concessions at Tientsin and Hankow in the same year. But what Germany most seriously required was a shipping and naval base, if possible with some rich territory around it. The German naval squadron, under the command of Rear-Admiral von Diederichs, whose regular function was to protect the new German Pacific islands and deal with troubles with the natives, was despatched to the Chinese coast to search for a suitable spot; like the French had acquired at Tonkin and the British at Hong Kong. After turning down Amoy, the Bay of Samsah and Fuchou, the German commander decided that the Bay of Kiaochau with the port of Tsingtau best suited German needs, especially as the province of Shantung inland was so rich in mineral wealth. The German Government began quietly enough by offering to buy the place from the Chinese, but there was no response to these overtures, beyond the sudden appearance of Chinese soldiers in the bay. By one of those happy chances which so often solve diplomatists' most delicate dilemmas, a pair of Catholic missionaries were murdered in the interior on November 1, 1897. 'We must take advantage of this excellent opportunity,' Kaiser Wilhelm II at once stated, 'before another great power either dismembers China or comes to her help! Now or never!' Von Diederichs was sent in with his men-of-war and some squadrons of cavalry. They met no resistance. By the treaty of March 6, 1898, the Governor of Shantung Province, who was held to be responsible for the murders, was deprived of office, the Chinese agreed 'to bestow a large indemnity in favour of the Catholic mission, and to promise the erection of three expiatory chapels'. At the same time, Germany was granted a 99-year lease of the Bay of Kiaochau and its immediate hinterland, together with the right to exploit the province's minerals and build railways to the mines.

It was to underline the terms of this treaty and to demonstrate the reality of German regal power ('to make clear to the Europeans in China, to the German merchants and, above all, to China herself,' as the Kaiser expressed it, 'that the German Michael has planted his shield firmly in the soil') that Prince Heinrich and the *Deutschland* led the German squadron to China. During March and April 1898 the squadron made powerful and stately progress up the Chinese coast; and von Spee wrote frequent letters home to the Countess describing in detail their reception by the Governors of Chinese provinces, and the royal salutes and the interminable banquets with which they were received. At the British colony of Hong Kong there were many festivities in honour of the Prince and his *entourage*. But there was also uneasy evidence of the international turmoil caused by the German seizure of Tsingtau. Russia had taken advantage of the opportunity to seize the vitally important strategic Port Arthur, which greatly displeased the British who seized Wei-hai-wei 'for as long as Russia holds Port Arthur'. Von Spee wrote that 'two Russian warships have suddenly just disappeared, and the whole British fleet leaves in a northerly direction. It is said that Russia will go for England, or the other way round. And the Americans seem to expect war with Spain.'

The German squadron cruised on to Tsingtau, where von Spee, always with an eye for natural history, deplored the lack of trees and greatly admired the flowers. The German soldiers were living in hovels previously occupied by the Chinese troops, but the town was already swarming with German civilians 'waiting for the purchase of land to be confirmed so that they can begin work'. He made an expedition inland to the frontier of the new German colony, which was heavily guarded 'in order to impress on the Chinese where our territory starts'. Later, at Peking there were receptions with the Emperor and Empress ('the first time she had seen a European') and sightseeing tours. There were ceremonial visits to demonstrate by the reality of German sea power the Kaiser's stake in China to the Russians at their newly acquired Port Arthur, and to the British at Wei-hai-wei. Wherever von Spee sailed he saw evidence of the intense international and nationalistic passions aroused by European and Asiatic preoccupation—however decorously conducted—with the colonization of China. The Russians sent out a prince, too, and Prince Cyril had to be entertained by Prince Heinrich with polo and hunting and banquets. In early October, a telegram from the German Ambassador in Peking told of riots against European interference. The Empress had imprisoned (and was going to poison) her son, the Emperor, ran the message, and the ambassador himself would like some military support. Crises alternated with festivities in bewildering succession. Even the Italians turned up in November in the 4,600-ton coast defence battleship *Marco Polo:* 'perhaps they are looking out for some territory for themselves', von Spee noted. Far away in Europe, and in Washington and nearer at hand in Tokyo, the machinery of power diplomacy was running at high speed as Lord Salisbury, Jules Ferry, Count Mouravieff, Kaiser Wilhelm II, President Theodore Roosevelt and the Mikado, among others who took a leading part in their country's foreign policy, jockeyed for position and territory. Britain and Japan were at loggerheads with Russia, Germany was the object of acute suspicion by everybody, France was carefully watching the balance of power everywhere, while America took more decisive action and sent Admiral Dewey to annihilate the Spanish Fleet in Manila Bay.

Before returning home to Germany, the *Deutschland* paid one last visit to Tsingtau to ensure that all was well. The results of German industry were already evident. New barracks for the occupying forces were under construction, and work was soon to begin on 'an entire Chinese village at some kilometres distant . . . to keep the native population as far as possible away'. Meanwhile, the natives were proving troublesome, not only, as von Spee observed, 'because they do not like hard work', but because a famine was raging and they did not care for the Germans anyway. 'The villages are quite empty,' von Spee reported after a tour of inspection; although in one of them the Chinese were really waiting in ambush for von Spee and his contingent. 'We managed to get away on foot, leaving all our luggage behind.'

Von Spee was to observe at first hand on several future occasions 'the price of Empire'. He returned home from the Far East in the summer of 1899, but was back again for the Boxer Rebellion in July of the following year, when all the colonial powers (Germany, France, Britain, Russia, America and Japan) joined forces to relieve their nationals besieged in the British legation in Peking after the assassination of the German Ambassador. Von Spee saw his first action up the Yangtsze river, found it curious that the Chinese should be fighting at all, but before returning home once more, was reassured by the tidiness and order he found at Tsingtau. Here the natives were under proper control, plans were being made for the construction of a great modern German city, and the first railway service to the riches of the interior had been inaugurated. In the Far East, German power and empire were being consolidated in a manner that would have warmed the heart of the late Chancellor Bismarck.

Germany's imperial responsibilities and ever-growing industrial and commercial power demanded an increasingly powerful fleet.

Through the decade of 1900 to 1910, the strength of the Imperial German Navy multiplied many times over and become a dominant factor in world power politics. The authority and rank of Maximilian von Spee rose in step with the service to which he had given his life. In 1905 he was promoted to the rank of captain. His first command was the battleship *Wittelsbach*, one of the numerous new German battleships which had led to the complete reappraisal of British defence policy and to British treaties of friendship with Japan and her old enemy, France, in mutual self-protection: Britain could no longer risk standing alone. Both Admiral Alfred von Tirpitz and Admiral Sir John Fisher concentrated the main strength of their navies in home waters, while squadrons of fast cruisers were assigned the task of protecting the German and British colonies in time of war. The British tended to rely on a larger number of heavier and older ships for this overseas duty, and the commanders were not usually of the first calibre. The Germans, on the other hand, sent their newest and fastest cruisers to Africa, the Far East and their Pacific colonies.

The most sought-after command in the Imperial German Navy was that of the East Asiatic Squadron, based on the now modern and thriving colony at Tsingtau. In peacetime, by tradition this was a crack squadron with a standard of efficiency unmatched in the service. Its responsibilities were manifold. In time of war, much would depend on the conduct and fighting prowess of this remote squadron. It was powerful enough to commit grievous damage to British warships in the Pacific, and to interrupt British trade to the Far East, the East Indies, India, Australia and New Zealand. Under no circumstances was it likely to succeed in fighting its way through the superior British fleet in European waters and back to Germany. Kaiser Wilhelm's instructions to the commanders of his cruisers in foreign waters should war break out were explicit:

'From that moment he must make his own decisions . . . Above all, the officer must bear in mind that his chief duty is to damage the enemy as severely as possible . . . The constant strain will exhaust the energy of his crew; the heavy responsibility of the officer in command will be increased by the isolated position of his ship; rumours of all kinds and the advice of apparently well-meaning persons will sometimes make the situation appear hopeless. But he must never show one moment of weakness. He must constantly bear in mind that the efficiency of the crew and their capacity to endure privations and dangers depend chiefly on his personality, his energy and the manner in which he does his duty. The more difficult and desperate the position, the more strictly the officer must adhere to the laws of military honour . . . If an officer in command succeeds in winning for his ship an honourable place in the history of the German Navy, I assure him of my Imperial favour . . .'

In November 1912 Maximilian von Spee was appointed to the prized command of the East Asiatic Squadron with the rank of Rear-Admiral. At fifty-one he had reached the summit of his long career in the navy. Since his first colonial cruise to West Africa twenty-eight years earlier he had matured into the traditional mould and form of a senior officer who has for long borne the lonely responsibilities of command at sea. He was more remote and austere and authoritative in his manner, and rather shy. He was moderate in his habits, although he would sometimes take a drink and smoke a cigar in the wardroom with his officers, when he enjoyed his game of bridge and philosophical and linguistic conversation. Best of all, if he could find someone interested in natural history (like one of his senior officers, Captain Maerker) he could talk with deep feeling and profound knowledge. This was an enthusiasm which had first been stirred in Africa and stimulated by the wide variety of natural life which he had observed in so many parts of the world during the creation of Germany's empire. A close friend and fellow-admiral wrote warmly of von Spee's simple, unaffected personality, and of the brave manner in which he faced the many formal occasions at which he had to be present and which he found so distasteful. 'He was not a brilliant speaker by nature, but he would speak clearly and concisely and without any notes, which might detract from the spontaneity of what he had to say.' This same contemporary wrote of his generosity, of his conservative taste in art ('he did not like anything too unusual or ugly'), of his deep loyalty to the Catholic faith, of his strictness as a disciplinarian. In appearance, he held himself as erectly as he had always done, and his great height made him immediately distinguishable on the bridge of his flagship. His hair, his short beard, his moustache and even his bushy eyebrows had all turned a steel-grey; his deep-set blue eyes suggested a fit man with instant reactions and a decisive mind. In battle, he would clearly be a formidable antagonist.

CHAPTER 2

Preparations for War

Maximilian von Spee arrived at Tsingtau to take up his command shortly before Christmas, 1912. For the next eighteen months he kept a diary and wrote regular letters home to his beloved wife. Besides his elder son Count Otto, his younger son Count Heinrich joined his father and brother at Tsingtau shortly afterwards. There are many references to the two boys in von Spee's letters, to their state of health and their professional progress, and to Otto's inherited enthusiasm for natural history.

The German East Asiatic Squadron rarely remained in one port for long. Its area of responsibility was immense, and although the ships could not hope in any one year to cover more than a fraction of it, they were on the move for much of the time—from Singapore to Rabaul, from Samoa to Guam and back again to Tsingtau via Yokohama. Sometimes they had to quell local uprisings (or just a show of arms might do), more often it was a matter of parades and receptions, speeches and banquets and balls. All the white colony were present at the Governor's reception for von Spee at Batavia. 'The women seemed a simple, unsophisticated lot. Only one seemed to have any pretensions to sophistication, a Mrs M, an American, I believe, and this had the effect of making her seem less enchanting than the others. . . . At 8 o'clock the members of the Government dined with me on board my flagship—the cool, brightly lit cabin, the iced drinks, and so on were welcomed by my guests. . . .'

Many of the receptions were followed by dances, decorous enough in the German colonies, more up-to-date when they were American or British. At Singapore 'the English officers and their ladies were quite wild, doing the newest American dances. . . . They are almost indecent'; while at Manila the Americans 'were really excellent at it, but everything is mixed up, Two-Step, One-Step and Tango, danced perfectly pleasantly by some, by others almost indecently. It needs supervision.' The Americans were also blamed for the inflated prices at Nagasaki. Von Spee went ashore to buy

Christmas presents for some of his fellow officers. 'I found they demanded outrageous prices. It is the fault of the Americans.' At Manila again there was an exceptionally large reception, arranged, to von Spee's annoyance, by the German consul. All von Spee wanted to do was to walk and climb in the country, and study the wildlife. Instead there was a great ball at the Army and Navy Club, where he was guest of honour. 'To my shame,' he confessed to his wife, 'I lied at least eight hundred times. You say "it is my greatest pleasure to meet you", while you are thinking how much better it would have been if they had stayed at home.' There were hundreds of guests. 'This hand-shaking is no joke.'

During the twenty months of his command before the war in Europe broke out there was a succession of carnivals, banquets and golf tournaments, formal receptions at Bangkok, race meetings at Hong Kong. Life was gay and busy among all the European colonial exiles; for the hierarchy the social round seemed never to cease, and the national barriers and conflicts of Europe were too remote to interfere with the important business of having a good time—mainly with ceremony and distinction among the officers and senior administrators and businessmen. But always von Spee, now promoted to Vice-Admiral, appears a reluctant participant, and always in his letters home there is evidence of the things closer to his heart—his affection for his family, his love for the country and the flowers and the trees, and his deep religious sentiments. Sadly he replies to a telegram telling of the death of his mother. 'I can only say how deeply grateful I am that God allowed her to be with us for so long. . . . I think of her with happiness as the best and most loyal mother one could imagine.' Proudly he writes of Otto's success as an officer, but quietly rebukes him for buying over-priced souvenirs; and of his younger brother: 'Heinrich is very well and seems to get on all right. He observes well, but does not express himself as vividly as Otto.' And he constantly refers to the flowers he finds ashore, and carries aboard to decorate his cabin. 'I brought some violets with me from Tsingtau. They are in full bloom and smell beautifully. Also I found some prickly plants with small white blossoms which smell marvellous.'

But there were, too, sterner occasions. Behind the brilliant façades—at Tsingtau, at Manila, at New Guinea, among the Caroline Islands—there were outbreaks of rebellion, which upset and puzzled von Spee, who set such a high store on order and cleanliness and firm discipline. Following an appeal from the Governor of New Guinea, he sailed his squadron to one of the Admiralty Islands to deal with 'the still unsettled population', where 'people taken prisoner are eaten', where 'they are black with long woolly hair (it seems to serve as a kind of handbag) and are suspicious of foreigners'. There had earlier been a particularly nasty uprising in the Carolines; von Spee had a stone monument inscribed with the names of the German dead and this was later hoisted aboard his flagship to be ceremonially erected at the scene of the battle.

The function of deterring and putting down rebellious natives was an important duty of von Spee's East Asiatic Squadron. But, if the point of detonation was likely to be 6,000 miles away in Europe, the prospect of imminent world war was never far from the admiral's mind. During the period of his command, the tradition of fighting efficiency of his squadron was strongly maintained. Away from the frivolities of life on shore, during their long cruises to the corners of the German eastern empire there was frequent gunnery and torpedo practice. The arduous and filthy business of coaling at sea in a Pacific swell was brought to a fine art. Evolutions were rehearsed time and again. Every possible tactical contingency was considered and planned for. Not only had the officers been carefully selected for this élite station; the men, too, were of the highest calibre, who took naturally to the severe discipline von Spee always imposed. The results were clear for all to see. There were no smarter ships serving in foreign water. 'The German Squadron . . . was like no other in the Kaiser's navy. It was commanded by professional officers and manned by long-service ratings,' wrote a British naval correspondent. The speed and accuracy of the squadron's shooting was a byword: for two successive years the East Asiatic Squadron won the Kaiser's Cup for the best marksmanship in the whole German navy.

In August 1914, the German East Asiatic Squadron was the most formidable single group of fighting ships of their class in the world. None of the men-of-war which von Spee commanded was more than eight years old, and all of them had been retained at their peak of fighting efficiency. His own flagship, the *Scharnhorst*, her hull painted white against the fierce eastern sun and protected by a six-inch belt of Krupp steel armour plate, was a purposeful-looking, four-funnelled cruiser of 11,600 tons, armed with eight 8·2-inch guns, each of which could hurl a 240-pound projectile over 13,000 yards, supported by six 5·9-inch guns in casemates and some twenty lighter weapons. The *Scharnhorst's* sister ship was the *Gneisenau*, a vessel of equal power and slightly greater speed; but for all practical purposes these two armoured cruisers were indistinguishable—among the finest of their breed in the world, fast enough to escape from any battleship, a match for any enemy cruiser, and destructible only by the newer, bigger and faster battle cruisers which had entered service since the German ships had first been commissioned. These two vessels formed the armoured core of Maximilian von Spee's squadron. Supporting them he had the light cruisers *Emden*, *Leipzig* and *Nürnberg*, fast, modern vessels, all capable of steaming at between 23 and 26 knots, all armed with ten 4·1-inch guns (this was a very formidable quick-firing weapon with a range of over 10,000 yards) and thinly protected by plating on their decks and conning tower. Together they made a neat, homogeneous unit, with the light cruisers acting as scouts and falling back on the heavy guns of the flagship and the *Gneisenau* if faced by a superior enemy. There were also seven gunboats and a torpedo boat, whose main function was to patrol the coastal regions and river estuaries of China for the protection of German territory, property leaseholds and trading posts.

In the second week of June 1914 little had occurred in Europe to suggest that war was any nearer than it had been for many anxious months past. At Tsingtau (a fine modern city now, with clean broad streets, handsome administrative buildings, neat houses for the German merchants, green parks, a racecourse even, and a complete well-defended naval harbour and dockyard) business was brisk, and most of the East Asiatic Squadron was in port. Two of the light cruisers were absent, the *Nürnberg* (with Otto von Spee on board) was still away on the Mexican coast guarding German interests against damage from the revolution which was raging there, while the *Leipzig* had recently been despatched to relieve her. The flagship of the British Far East Fleet, the armoured cruiser *Minotaur*, flying the flag of Vice-Admiral Sir Thomas Jerram, had arrived on a courtesy visit to the German base, with the inevitable exchange of courtesies followed by a round of balls and dinners and friendly sports. The British sailors won the football match, a German team from the *Scharnhorst* proved their superiority at the tug-o'-war. The atmosphere was most cordial, and the Germans were sorry to say goodbye to the British cruiser on June 16th: they had always got on so well together. Plans had been completed for the summer round of state visits and the showing-the-flag 'through the German sphere of influence'. It was to be a long voyage for the two big cruisers. They were to proceed first to Nagasaki, then in a majestic grand cruise of the German Pacific empire to the Mariana and Caroline Islands, Samoa, returning by Suva in the Fiji group, the Bismarck Archipelago and Kaiser Wilhelmsland in New Guinea. En route they would ceremonially erect the memorial to the German dead at Ponapé.

Although the climate of Tsingtau was almost perfect, the crews of both ships were looking forward to their summer outing. When they returned on September 20th, many of them would have completed their two years overseas service, and were due to return home by train across Siberia to their families for Christmas. Spirits were therefore high. It was a day of brilliant sunshine, and as the great white-hulled *Gneisenau* cast off and slowly steamed in a wide circle out of the harbour, watched from the shore by comrades and groups of dockyard coolies, she gave an impression of stately strength and grandeur. From the armoured cruiser's decks and beneath the long barrels of her guns voices rose in chorus singing *Wem Gott will rechte Gunst erweisen, den schickt er in die weite Welt.* 'At the horseshoe reef,' wrote the ship's first officer, 'we hoisted the last boat and then passed the Ju-nui-san lighthouse, which separated the inner and outer roads. After exchanging, off Arkona Island, a last signal with the shore, we parted from this pleasant corner of the world. .... The three peaks of the Prinz Heinrich mountain receded, the Kaiserstuhl faded from sight, and only the Lauschan, jutting out of the sea, long remained visible to us, like a defiant guardian.'

After a brief call at Nagasaki, where coal was taken on board and the last mail from home was awaiting them, the *Gneisenau*—soon to be joined by von Spee and the *Scharnhorst*—sailed south into the tropics. Day by day it became hotter. Awnings were spread as protection against the burning sun and the sailors were ordered to wear their wide-brimmed straw hats after they crossed the Tropic of Cancer on June 26th. In the evenings it was still desperately hot below the cruiser's steel decks, and the men would come up with their chess boards and their musical instruments and sing songs of home 'where the fields were now ripening in the fine summer heat'. The darkness, which brought relief to those on board, also greatly increased the range and quality of reception of the messages from the German wireless stations, so painstakingly built up in an intricate inter-connecting web across the German Pacific empire. On the night of June 29th the ether was specially congested with overlapping messages in several languages. Far away in Europe, it seemed, the Archduke Franz Ferdinand of Austro-Hungary and his wife had been assassinated at Sarajevo. 'Now into our fight drill,' wrote Commander Hans Pochhammer of the *Gneisenau*, 'which we had been zealously carrying out all this time, was imparted a touch of a more serious flavour, and a kind of subconscious feeling that we were approaching a difficult time.'

There was no further news of the crisis in Europe at Saipan, where there were exchange visits with the natives, which were a common practice, a mutual expression of loyalty, during these island visits. Here there was a call on the local school, where the native children rose from their desks when the officers entered their hut, and showed how well they were learning their German lessons, both in prose and in verse. This was followed by a visit to a settlement of Samoans, living on the island in enforced exile after their bloody rebellion three years earlier, and a return call from this tribe, 'the men and the village maidens dancing and singing on the quarterdeck, after rubbing themselves with palm oil'. Occasions such as these seemed to confirm the benevolence as well as the enduring strength of the German empire; it might have already lasted a thousand years instead of less than thirty.

After sailing through the edge of a typhoon, the two big cruisers arrived at Truk, edging their way carefully through the reef and into the calm lagoon. Coaling began again the following evening, the *Scharnhorst* and *Gneisenau* vying with one another for the speed and efficiency in carrying out this task. There had been a time—and in 1914 it was only a half-century ago—when fighting ships could sail the oceans of the world for indefinite periods, dependent on bases and anchorages only for provisions and water, and perhaps the replacement of a sail or a spar or the scraping of crustaceans from the underside of the hull. All this had changed with the coming of the first screw frigates, the ancestors of Admiral von Spee's cruisers. Now the endurance of a fighting ship was measured in days or a few thousand miles. The *Scharnhorst* had a capacity of 2,000 tons of coal for her 26,000 horsepower vertical inverted triple expansion engines. At economical speed she burnt nearly 100 tons a day; at higher speed she would consume close to 500 tons a day. At 10 knots she could sail for over 5,000 miles without refuelling, but like the driver of a car, the captain would be looking for fuel long before this distance had been covered; at 20 knots the *Scharnhorst*'s bunkers would be empty after four-and-a-half days, having covered only 2,200 miles. For a coal-burning navy there had to be coaling bases, defended by guns and protected by garrisons of troops, wherever it might have to operate. Colliers had to be constantly re-stocking these bases. The radius of action and the operating efficiency of every warship was conditioned by the need for coal, and even a single warship on a long cruise away from its base had to bring with it, like vulnerable satellites, its own colliers. These restricted both its speed and operational efficiency. Alternatively, the warship had to arrange complicated rendezvous far ahead in time and distance. Coal was a bugbear and a bore to every naval commander. To the men, coaling was an inescapable hardship of life at sea. It was a back-breaking, filthy job under the best conditions— at Tsingtau before they sailed there had been fixed coaling derricks as well as hundreds of coolies to help, but still the men were thankful when it was over, and it had taken hours to clean down the ships with hoses. The effect of coaling was always to negate one of the first principles of good seamanship, that of keeping the vessel trim and tidy, clean and polished. Coal dust seeped everywhere, into the guns' delicate sighting mechanism, into the men's clothing, and it left a filthy black film over scrubbed decks and highly polished brass.

Coaling was an uncomfortable undertaking in the full heat of a tropical sun. At Truk, von Spee ordered that it was to be conducted during the evening and the early part of the night, and a Japanese collier and the German armed collier, *Titania*, a permanent unit of the East Asiatic Squadron, came alongside the anchored armoured cruisers and made fast for the transfer of their cargoes. Soon the white steam from the derrick donkey engines rose from the decks of the colliers, blended with the grey pall of coal dust and drifted slowly above the lagoon. Across the water to the natives lining the shore came the unfamiliar sounds of rattling chains and cables, of labouring engines, and the cries and occasional hearty songs of German seamen working hard. When darkness fell lamps were lit above the emptying holds of the colliers and, in mutual illumination, each of the sister fighting ships played its searchlights on the decks of the other. In coaling, there was always competition, but there must also always be comradely co-operation.

But Truk offered joys and pleasures too, the last peaceful and carefree recreation most of the officers and men were to experience. When the bunkers were full and the ships cleaned down, there followed days when parties could explore ashore or sail among the beautiful islands. For von Spee himself, this was a paradise of natural life, from rare mammals and fishes to multitudes of birds and butterflies of all sizes and colours. Then late one afternoon a party of natives came aboard the flagship 'to dance before the great German chief'. Von Spee ceremonially received the chieftains from an armchair on the quarterdeck, asking after their welfare and that of their white officials, while the flagship's company squatted for the show in their hundreds on the after 8·2-inch gun turret, on the upper works and on the mainmast abaft the fourth of the great funnels. Coconut mats were spread out, one for each tribe, and then in turn and to the sound of the clapping hands and the slapping of thighs and the rattle of tortoise-shell earrings, 'the sinewy figures, rubbed with palm oil, moved rhythmically in the sunlight'. The girls followed, to the special delight of the men, as dusk fell, and then at last in the tropical night the tribes made their way back home, their canoes twinkling with the flames of many torches, and the searchlights of the cruisers making patterns across the lagoon and pointing white guiding fingers to their destination. It had been a spirited and happy evening, 'and the squadron chief was visibly pleased'.

On the following night the searchlights were put to sterner use. The wireless signals told of a worsening political situation in Europe. There was talk of mobilization in Austro-Hungary and Russia, and the real possibility of war. The *Scharnhorst* and *Gneisenau* put to sea, and the guns thundered out in practice against a towed target, while at night the men again were called to battle stations and the searchlights flashed from ship to ship in mock combat. The efficiency of the East Asiatic Squadron was as high as ever. Von Spee was pleased with the results, and signalled his congratulations. There still remained time for the commander-in-chief to indulge his enthusiasm for natural history. The little atoll of Oroluk which they passed was famous for its rare tortoises and the two warships hove to, von Spee speeding ashore in his white pinnace to see what he could find. There were none. Instead, he discovered a Japanese fishing schooner, an innocent enough sight at any other time, but in these critical days might she not be there

39

for a more sinister purpose? Japan, which had built up a powerful navy in the Pacific, had a treaty of friendship with Britain, and the whereabouts of the German squadron would be a subject of acute interest in Tokyo as well as in London.

No one but von Spee and his staff knew that their destination was Ponapé, the seat of the German Government in the Caroline Islands. Ponapé was one of the most recent colonial acquisitions, a part of the spoils of the Spanish-American war of 1898, and purchased from a defeated Spain 'to safeguard Germany's interests in the Carolines as far as possible and in a powerful manner'. Spain had at first been reluctant to yield up this rich territory, but the state of this defeated nation's finances was as precarious as her colonial empire. The inevitability of the change of ownership had been sadly underlined in the inaugural speech of the Spanish Cortes by the Queen Regent in June 1899, when she had emphasized that 'the most important, urgent and difficult task imposed upon you by your mandate is to balance our finances'. She had spoken, too, of 'all the sorrows which have afflicted our hearts in consequence of the misfortunes of our country' and lamented that 'the diminished remains of our former Empire' must go. The invaluable naval base at Guam—together with the Philippines and all her western empire—had of course already gone to the victors. Now, Spain was in no position to refuse Germany's offer of 16,750,000 marks (or £837,000) for the Carolines, Pelew and the Marianas. These had passed into German hands on October 1, 1899: a bargain although a very troublesome one. The natives of Ponapé especially—they were mostly of Malay origin—had been resentful of Spanish rule, and liked their new masters rather less because they seemed so busy and industrious and were always making them build roads into the interior, which deprived them of their privacy and spoilt the hunting. The tribes of the little island of Jokoz hated the Germans most and murdered some of them late in the year of 1910. The first reinforcements of ninety men had proved inadequate, and in the end three East Asiatic Squadron cruisers had to be sent. There was a full-scale bombardment and assault before the 250 tribesmen were killed or captured. Fifteen more were then shot and the rest of the tribe banished to Yap where they could be properly supervised: a punishment the justice of which, the senior officer of the punitive expedition reported, 'the natives are said to recognize'.

Peace had reigned at Ponapé since then. But the East Asiatic

1 The two adversaries at the Battle of Coronel, Vice-Admiral von Spee (*left*) and Rear-Admiral Cradock (*Imperial War Museum*)

2 Von Spee's flagship, SMS *Scharnhorst* (*Imperial War Museum*)

3 Captain von Müller's light cruiser *Emden* (*Imperial War Museum*)

4 The *Nürnberg* at Honolulu embarking stores

5 The East Asiatic Squadron meets heavy seas in the Pacific (*Süddeutscher Verlag*)

Squadron had not forgotten the occasion, for it had marked the first fighting many of them had seen. That was why the flagship bore the commemorative stone inscribed with the names of the German dead and wounded for erection in the churchyard.

The mountains of Ponapé came into sight at noon on July 17th, hanging like grey-brown clouds above the green of the lower forests and encircled on the ocean by a white ring of raging spray of the outer reef. The *Scharnhorst* anchored off the island of Jokoz, now settled by less intransigent Mortlock natives, where the German flag floated reassuringly from the mast outside the Jaluit Company's offices. It was a serenely beautiful scene. The admiral was soon ashore, eager to pursue his two warmest enthusiasms, natural history and the art of war. There was wildlife of all kinds on Jokoz as well as the evidence of recent combat. Here was the line of the trench the insurgents had dug, there the caves where they had sheltered against the cruisers' bombardment. Maximilian von Spee examined them with professional interest. The brave bluejackets had forced their way, dragging a machine gun, up this precipitous slope, through the tangled brush which further protected the natives. It was no wonder that the assault had led to casualties before the shells and Mauser bullets had at length defeated the Jokoz rebels. And there, on the summit, was the wooden cross, as evidence that the victory had not been won without cost. The view that met the eyes of von Spee and his party was a magnificent reward for their climb. The spread of mangroves and palm trees was broken by the red-roofed huts of the peaceful natives; their fishing canoes were in the blue lagoon. 'Our proud ships were lying peacefully at anchor,' observed a senior officer. And beyond the bright white annulus of the reef separating the still waters from the Pacific rollers, the ocean stretched to the horizon.

The ceremony of erection of the memorial stone in the church-yard, performed with dignity by von Spee after his tour of the battlefield, should have completed the squadron's stay at Ponapé. Instead, they were delayed for several days for it had suddenly become too dangerous to move. Here at Ponapé they had direct communications with the outside world. Every night brought worse news from Europe: Austro-Hungary had sent an ultimatum to Serbia, and three days later had declared war; Russia was mobilizing her armies, Germany was demanding that she demobilize them. Von Spee ordered his ships to prepare for war, only as a drill, of course. It was something they had done many times before in the course of exercises. Not one of the sailors believed this was just a drill for word gets round swiftly on shipboard. Until July 28th parties had been allowed ashore, to swim and climb and explore inland. There had even been some games, all played in an atmosphere of uneasy expectation. Then shore leave was halted. Von Spee inspected his flagship for war readiness. He was grave but satisfied. These men worked well and they would fight well; he never had any doubt of that. His pinnace took him across the lagoon to the *Gneisenau* where he was piped on board and taken on a brisk tour of inspection by Captain Maerker, one of his closest friends in the squadron, and a fellow natural historian and bridge partner. All was well.

Nothing happened for forty-eight hours. The sun rose blood-red beyond the reef, climbed high across the blue sky until it was poised vertically above the two white ships, pouring its heat down through the steel armoured decks. Drill was kept to a minimum. Beneath the shelter of their awnings, the men smoked and watched the natives fish from their canoes. This, surely, was the still, awful lull before Armageddon—a hundred times more threatening than the silence that preceded a Pacific typhoon. On July 31st the word came through, circuitously by cable and wireless from the other half of the world: 'Threatened state of war.' Germany's twelve-hour ultimatum to Russia was running out.

This time there was no attempt to disguise the reality of the situation. The ships were to be stripped for war: those were the admiral's orders. Lighters were towed out from the little harbour and came alongside and for hour after hour, through the heat of the midday sun, were loaded with the inflammable and vulnerable decorations and comforts that were essential for the well-being of officers and men in peacetime, but a hazard in battle. Wood panelling and tapestries were torn from the bulkheads of the wardrooms and thrown overboard into the lagoon, the more colourful fragments to be seized upon by natives and taken back by canoe to decorate their huts. Sofas and armchairs, pictures (that of the Kaiser was spared) and pianos, carpets and sideboards were stacked on deck. The captain's silver service and fine crockery were crated up and marked. Except for the admiral's, the officers' formal uniform, resplendent in gold braid and piping, was folded carefully away in cabin trunks and stacked democratically alongside the men's kit-bags to await stowage into the lighters. In the men's quarters the lockers yielded a vast collection of prized mementoes: vases in bronze and porcelain, Japanese temple lanterns, ivory carvings, buddhas and weapons and curios—each one a memory of the Orient, all of them a random cross-section of every noisy bazaar from Singapore to Nagasaki. 'The whole beautiful world through which we had passed . . . flashed before us as we packed away all these treasures in quickly-prepared cases,' wrote one officer. 'Many a pious wish to parents, brothers, sisters, wives and children were packed away with them, and the hope crept in that we might be at home to see them unpacked.'

The expected news arrived in von Spee's cabin late on the evening of August 2nd. Mobilization had been ordered against both France and Russia. It was too late to assemble the crews; better that they should get a good night's rest after their day's labours and in preparation for what might lie ahead. Instead, his own flag captain and Captain Maerker would address their men at dawn. It was a still, sultry night, full of the urgent signals of war, among them messages to the nearest British warships. The following morning, the captain's rousing speeches to their ship's companies were followed in turn by three cheers for the Kaiser, and then by the appearance of von Spee, tall, erect, authoritative and fiercely self-confident, the embodiment of heroism and leadership. In the *Gneisenau* he climbed up on to the crown of the after 8·2-inch gun turret to address his men and their officers, among them his son Heinrich. You must all, he told them, make good your oaths in the service of Emperor and Empire. 'At the moment, only Russia and France are our enemies, England's attitude is still uncertain, although hostile. We must therefore regard all English ships as enemy ships. . . .'

Confirmation was soon received that Britain had indeed joined her allies, and that Germany was at war on land on two fronts, and that at sea she faced the might of the Royal Navy. Against the French and Russian naval forces in the Pacific von Spee possessed greatly superior strength. The combined British and Australian squadrons were another matter altogether. His two principal adversaries were Admiral Jerram, to whom he had offered such warm hospitality only a month earlier, and Rear-Admiral Sir George Patey. Against Jerram alone, he stood a good chance of victory. Besides his flagship, *Minotaur*, the equal in power and size and speed to either of von Spee's big cruisers, Jerram had under his command an older armoured cruiser, two modern light cruisers (more than a match for any of von Spee's), a handful of destroyers, submarines and gunboats, and an old slow battleship in dock and demobilized at Hong Kong. He was also promised the support of Rear-Admiral A. L. M. Huguet's two rather tired old French armoured cruisers. The toughest opposition lay far to the south, at Sydney and Brisbane in Australia. Here Admiral Patey flew his flag in the modern Dreadnought battle cruiser, *Australia*, a faster and bigger ship than the *Gneisenau* and *Scharnhorst*. In open battle this flagship alone could in theory choose the range against both German ships and pulverize them with her 12-inch shells (each three-and-a-half times heavier than the Germans' heaviest) without receiving a hit in reply. Against this great 19,000-ton fighting ship von Spee would be helpless. To scout for him and perhaps also to destroy the weaker German light cruisers, Patey possessed in the *Sydney* and *Melbourne* two of the fastest light cruisers in the world, armed with 6-inch guns (against the Germans' 4·1-inch); two older light cruisers, and more destroyers and submarines. Well handled and undistracted by other duties, these combined forces must in the end track down von Spee and bring him to battle. They had so much on their side, besides *matériel* superiority. They had permanent, invulnerable bases in Australia and New Zealand, at Singapore, Hong Kong and Wei-hai-wei, with ample coal and docking facilities. Time was on their side, and cable and wireless had revolutionized the art of hunting down a foe at sea. Von Spee had only one fortified base in the whole German Pacific empire, and if he retreated to Tsingtau he would at once be blockaded in and eventually sunk at his moorings, as the Russians had been destroyed at Port Arthur ten years earlier. His coaling problems were a logistical nightmare. How could he hope to keep his bunkers full? And even if he met and defeated an inferior searching force, his ammunition would be irreplaceable and his damage irreparable. Time and the chances of fate must surely catch up with him in the end.

But Maximilian von Spee possessed certain real advantages, too. First, there was the quality of his men and his ships. Most of his men had been with him for a long time and were a tightly trained, intensely loyal team. Their skill with their guns was a by-word throughout the naval world. Tactically, they had all the advantages of the hunted in a vast ocean. They might disappear without trace for weeks, raiding the trade routes for colliers, bombarding a shore installation at dusk and disappearing at high speed into the night. They could divide their forces, prey upon defenceless merchantmen from Chile to Singapore, and rendezvous at some remote atoll. Fear, and impossibly high insurance rates, could bring all trade in the Pacific and Indian oceans to a standstill, and prevent the sailing to Europe of the armies of Australia, New Zealand and India. Von Spee could seriously influence the course of the war in Europe, without even firing a shot. All he had to do was to survive. But his chances of survival must greatly diminish, and the Pacific must soon become untenable, if the Japanese navy entered the arena.

In the summer of 1914 Japan, recovered now from the economic depression that had followed her victory over Russia a decade before, had completed the first phase of her massive naval programme. The Imperial Japanese Navy could field in the Pacific nearly a dozen battleships and battle cruisers, some of them of the most modern type and including the biggest and most powerful battle cruiser in the world. Japan was bound by a treaty of friendship with Britain, but was not required to come to her aid in a European war. Perhaps she would remain neutral, ready to pick up the spoils from the defeated and the weakened victors. Perhaps she would decide to move in on the German colonies, especially Tsingtau, which she must surely covet.

Maximilian von Spee was ready for the responsibilities that faced him on August 6, 1914. He had had many months to prepare for most of the eventualities that might arise in time of war and had laid his plans accordingly. Elaborate directions for the conduct of cruiser warfare had been drawn up in Berlin. But with the declaration of hostilities there was little more that his superiors could do to assist him: the German High Seas Fleet was keeping to its bases; except in the Pacific, the German navy had ceased to have any influence on maritime events. 'From now on,' as the admiral wrote in his diary, 'I am on my own.' Early in the afternoon of August 6th, he went ashore with his two sons and together they made their way to the Catholic Mission. Bishop Salvator Walleser O.M.Cap., Apostolic Vicar of the Marianas and Carolines, was awaiting them to hear their confession. All the family received the holy sacrament very devoutly, according to the bishop: 'Their marvellous example made a deep impression on everybody.'

The admiral returned to his cabin to complete his plans. Already much had been accomplished. The *Nürnberg* had been recalled from San Francisco fifteen days earlier and had hurried back by way of Honolulu to rejoin the flag. The *Emden*, too, had been recalled, and would soon join them. Already they were more powerful both in spiritual and *matériel* strength. The two big armoured ships were in fighting trim and ready for battle, stripped of all non-essentials. Below, raw steel bulkheads and decks, and naked lamps hanging starkly from their wires, emphasized the readiness for combat. Even the little *Titania* with her single gun and precious load of 2,000 tons of coal had hoisted the German naval flag: henceforth she would be SMS *Titania*.

The *Titania* was singled out for the honour of leading the East Asiatic Squadron out to sea, and to war. Perkily she steamed across the lagoon at 4 p.m., black smoke belching from her single thin funnel, through the gap in the reef and out into the Pacific. The flagship followed, then the *Gneisenau*, and finally the *Nürnberg*. Their destination was to the north, to Pagan in the Marianas, 1,000 miles away. To this island von Spee had summoned not only the *Emden*, but as many colliers, supply ships and liners as he could muster. Pagan would be their first temporary base, where the plans for cruiser warfare could be completed and where coaling and provisioning could be carried out. The last news from Berlin of Japan's likely intentions was clear if cryptic: 'Japan will remain neutral.' The richest area, then, for British, French and Russian trade was along the Chinese coast. This was where they would go. And if they met Jerram and his cruisers, von Spee had no doubts of the outcome.

CHAPTER 3

The Long Voyage

This first night at sea, on August 6, 1914, marked the beginning of the East Asiatic Squadron's Pacific odyssey. First the cries of farewell from the native canoes, then the thunder of the breakers on Ponapé's reef, faded behind them. It was a marvellous tropical night and it was no hardship for the men off watch to be sleeping fully dressed by their searchlights and guns. Lights were masked and the progress of the Squadron was marked only by the long trails of black smoke from the funnels above and the contrasting phosphorescent white of their wakes. By day, the sun was fiercer than they had ever experienced before, and they were without the protection of their awnings, which were considered a fire danger and had been left behind. At Divine service in the *Gneisenau* on the morning of August 6th, the heat was almost unbearable and no metal part on the exposed decks could be touched for long by human flesh without burning. The congregation assembled in their white uniforms and straw hats, the chaplain in his white surplice without his gown. A merciful breath of breeze brought temporary relief from their suffering. 'By God's help,' intoned the chaplain, 'shall we perform deeds. Thus we are strong without, stout of heart, faithful in service . . .' The assembled company found it very affecting.

The twin volcanic peaks of Pagan rose above the horizon at dawn on August 11th. Soon the anchorage became the gathering point for many of the largest German merchantmen and liners which had been caught at sea by the war and then hastened both to nourish and seek the protection of von Spee's powerful squadron. The Lloyd liner *Yorck* was already there. The collier *Staatssekretär Kraetke* arrived soon after the warships. Then from above the horizon black smudges of smoke marked the appearance of more German ships—the *Holsatia*, the slender little *Longmore*, the impressive *Prinz Waldemar*. And the heavier metal, too: the formidable armed liner—now an auxiliary cruiser—the *Prinz Eitel Friedrich*, disguised as a British P and O liner. The *Titania*, ever eager for duties and patrolling to and fro outside the anchorage, checked credentials, and allowed in the motley assortment one by one. There was one ship, familiar in silhouette and fierce in demeanour, that was indisputably a welcome friend. The light cruiser *Emden* had arrived safely from Tsingtau. And she had good news. The *Emden* had drawn first blood. She had captured the Russian Volunteer Fleet steamer *Riasan*, halted by threatening shots across her bows, in the Straits of Korea. She was welcomed by cheers from the men lining the rails of the *Scharnhorst* and *Gneisenau*.

At Pagan there was an embarrassment of riches for von Spee's squadron before they went off to war. Besides military supplies and coal in thousands of tons, there were provisions of all kinds, from live cattle and pigs to fresh vegetables and flour, biscuits and preserves, beer and wine, whisky and tobacco. At least they would live well for a while. But for how long? In the cruiser squadron there were more than 2,000 officers and men for whom food and fresh water had to be provided. Fresh water for the boilers, as well as oil and grease for the engines, were continuously consumed at sea; while hundreds of tons of coal would be daily burnt not only in the warships, but in the colliers, too, which would follow behind with the reserve supplies of their vital fuel like packhorse fodder. But four expected supply ships had failed to arrive at Pagan, one of them carrying the last of the mail from home, which had arrived at Tsingtau since their departure. This was an especially bitter blow for the men.

Every one of these lost ships had been intercepted and captured by the enemy, early evidence of the fearful supply hazards that lay ahead for the admiral. However he might contrive to send messages to German naval agents (who had, like British agents, long before been established in all important neutral ports), the likely destination of every neutral collier and merchantman would be noted by the British and the news would arrive at the Admiralty in London within hours. The German island colonies must soon fall, and with them would disappear the cable and wireless stations—at Apia, Yap, Rabaul and other islands—leaving von Spee with only his ships' wireless, a means of communication that was unpredictable in range and dangerously revealing of his whereabouts. (The German Telefunken wireless was, however, greatly superior to the enemy's.) Only a resounding victory over the enemy offered von Spee a respite, for this would soften neutral opinion in his favour, allow him to interpret generously the international laws governing the use of neutral harbours and dockyards, and give him temporary control of the seas about him. That was why his plan was to continue north from Pagan and, by preying on British shipping, hope to entice Jerram's cruiser force within range of his guns. He had no doubt whatever that he could outshoot his old friend if he met him before Patey's powerful forces in Australia joined him.

All these plans, which offered survival, and perhaps glory too, had to be cast away on the following day, August 12th, when a message from Tsingtau brought news of a sudden change in the attitude of Japan. At Tokio the decision had been reached that if Britain and Australia were going to seize Germany's Pacific empire then Japan must have her shares of the spoil, too. The colony of Kiaochau, the rich minerals of Shantung, and above all the modern naval base of Tsingtau, were all ripe for the picking. So, an ultimatum was despatched to Berlin: Yield up your Chinese colony peacefully, or we shall go to war.

Von Spee ordered a meeting of his commanders on board his flagship, including the captain of the powerful armed liner *Prinz Eitel Friedrich*. In his cabin in the *Scharnhorst* the admiral, with his staff in attendance, outlined the situation with the aid of a large map of the Pacific. War with Japan appeared inevitable. A part of her powerful navy would be needed for the attack on Tsingtau, but the rest must join the hunt for them. Japan's naval bases would then be available to the enemy, and the weight of power both from Japan in the north and from Australia in the south would be overwhelming. Even the most skilful seamanship, the most ardent fighting spirit and the most accurate gunfire could not hope to prevail against these forces of fast, modern men-of-war ranged against them. A further mutilated message from Tsingtau had since arrived, von Spee announced. 'Report from Tokyo,' it read. 'Declaration of war . . . enemy fleet apparently proceeding to the south . . .' And yet another message told of Jerram taking his squadron south and east from Hong Kong to destroy the German wireless station at Yap. All this evidence pointed with agonizing clarity to one simple tactical conclusion: a steel trap was closing about the German cruisers, from the south, from the west, and from the north.

The five captains, hatless and in white duck uniform, flanked von Spee who stood before his chart table while he developed his theme. We must maintain our squadron together as a single unit, he told them. The longer we can conceal our whereabouts and our intentions, the greater will be the enemy's confusion and the more ships he will have to deploy against us. Every warship that takes up the hunt against us means a proportionate weakening of the enemy force threatening our fleet at home. Fuel is our main difficulty. If we proceed to the Indian Ocean, where we could play havoc with trade and threaten the troop convoys from India and Australia (thus bringing relief to our brave armies fighting in Europe), we shall be faced with the impossibility of obtaining coal. We have no coaling bases in that area, and no agents with whom we can get in touch. Regretfully, then, we must put aside the idea of a raid to the west. I have decided, after careful consideration, to sail east across the Pacific to the coast of America. Here we have friends. We have agents from San Francisco to Punta Arenas in the Magellan Straits who can arrange for coal supplies and provisions. Chile especially is a friendly neutral and we may even be able to get docking facilities. But above all, we shall raid our enemies' trade routes and cut off supplies of food to Britain and halt the flow of phosphates and saltpetre to the shell factories of our enemies, France and Britain.

This was the theme of the Commander-in-Chief's announcement to his commanders. Then he turned to them. 'What is your view of the situation, gentlemen?'

In turn, von Spee's own flag-captain, Captain Maerker of the *Gneisenau*, Captain Thiereken of the *Prinz Eitel Friedrich* and Captain Karl von Schönberg of the *Nürnberg* nodded and expressed their agreement. Only Karl von Müller of the *Emden* hesitated. The fighting tradition went back far in this officer's ancestry. His own father and both his grandfathers had fought with the Prussian and German armies, and his family were noted for their extreme nationalistic views. Von Müller had achieved rapid promotion in the navy, reaching the rank of Korvettenkapitan at the age of only 35, and succeeded in acquiring both medals for bravery and privileged appointments to the most senior officers in his service. It was typical of von Müller that he had been the first to strike a blow against the enemy, and numbered among his officers the Kaiser's nephew Prince Franz Joseph von Hohenzollern. He expected special treatment as a matter of course, and was prepared to speak his mind, even to von Spee.

'I am afraid, sir,' said von Müller, 'that we shall be able to do practically nothing during a long cruise in the Pacific, and I am not so sure as you are that much value should be attached to the "fleet-in-being" theory. If you consider that there are too many difficulties against coaling the whole squadron in East Asian, Australian and Indian waters, would you consider permitting me to operate alone in the Indian Ocean?'

The accounts on this stage of the conference are not clear on what followed, but it would seem likely that von Spee was taken aback by the suggestion and was preparing to oppose it before his own chief of staff, Captain Fielitz, offered his opinion in support of von Müller. Von Spee agreed to consider the idea, even though it would mean the loss of one of his two light cruisers.

Von Müller returned to his ship, where coaling had just been completed. The men were slaking their thirst on a load of coconuts brought aboard by a shore party. He did not have to wait long for his admiral's decision. Shortly afterwards, a launch from the flagship came alongside with the message from von Spee that von Müller's request had been granted.

That night von Spee was to write in his diary: 'A single light cruiser which consumes far less coal and can, if necessary, coal from captured steamships, will be able to maintain herself longer than the whole squadron in the Indian Ocean; and as there are great prizes to be won there, it seems advisable to dispatch our fastest light cruiser . . . with our best collier.'

On the evening of August 14th the last preparations for the long voyage across the Pacific had been completed. Oxen and pigs had been slaughtered by the score and hoisted aboard the cruisers, and the Chinese laundrymen had gone. Their impeccable washing and ironing would be sadly missed by the officers. So would the brave foreman himself. 'Captain, I'm not afraid, I want to stay,' he appealed. 'Of course this was unavailing,' Captain Maerker recorded, 'and the pigtails had to leave. We embarked them, with a couple of bags of rice, on a coastal steamer . . .'

Ten days after the declaration of war against Germany by Britain, von Spee sailed from Pagan in dirty weather with his squadron and his mixed fleet train. His course was south-east, his next port of call Eniwetok Atoll in the Marshall Islands. But only a handful of his senior officers knew their destination. Absolute secrecy was vital to the success of their mission to America. There was to be strict wireless silence, no rubbish was to be thrown overboard in case, by a million-to-one chance, it should be spotted in the vast wastes of the Pacific, picked up and identified. They sailed in two columns, the

Scharnhorst leading the cruisers formed to port, a neat and awesome line of white hulls and bristling gun barrels; the merchantmen to starboard, headed by the *Prinz Eitel Friederich*, in an untidy and irregular line of chipped black and red painted dirty funnels and iron plating and cluttered decks. During the night the wind increased, all semblance of formation among the merchantmen in the darkness was lost, only the *Titania* and the big *Prinz Eitel Friedrich* holding their stations. At dawn the *Nürnberg* was despatched to round up the stragglers and fretfully nurse them back into line.

The sudden departure of the *Emden* later in the morning came as a surprise to almost everyone. She swung out of line, flashing a last signal by lamp to her flagship. 'I thank your Excellency for the confidence placed in me. I wish the cruiser Squadron a successful cruise.' 'Good luck,' replied von Spee; and almost at once the warship and her attendant collier had disappeared into the mist and squally rain.

The awareness of loneliness and of being abandoned by friends and of being hunted by the enemy was especially acute after the departure of the *Emden* on her raiding mission. It was not only the melancholy weather and that their strength had been reduced by the loss of one of their scouts. Correct though their commander's decision must be, it could not be denied that they were abandoning their policy of aggression and, if not retreating, withdrawing from the area where they were most likely to meet the foe. Lucky *Emden*! Soon there would be fighting for her, while they sailed on in silence, fearful of every smudge of smoke on the horizon. They were a 'fleet-in-being', and they must remain only a hidden threat. It was all very disappointing.

At the Admiralty in Berlin little hope was held out for von Spee's survival. It could be only a matter of time before he must succumb to the great forces already hunting for him. 'The news of Japan's impending entry into the war makes its position hopeless,' ran the text of a Naval Staff Assessment, which concluded with the fateful words, 'It is better to send no instructions to the Commander-in-Chief; the Kaiser might, however, send a message of encouragement.' Kaiser Wilhelm accepted this suggestion. 'God be with you in the impending stern struggle. My thoughts accompany you,' he signalled. But these royal good wishes were never received. The East Asiatic Squadron was already beyond the range of the radio transmitter at Tsingtau, so soon to fall before the bayonets and *banzai* cries of Japanese soldiers.

Maximilian von Spee was spared one burden which added such a weight to the responsibilities of his enemy. Berlin had decided that its East Asiatic commander 'must have complete liberty of action'— sagacious advice under the circumstances, and especially considering that all hope of communicating rapidly with him must soon end. His enemy, however, was to enjoy no such freedom. In centuries of British sea fighting, from the Armada to Trafalgar, the fame and glory had gone to the fighting admiral, who conducted his campaigns far from the seat of administrative power in London. New means of communication had altered all that. In 1914 the rulers at the Admiralty in London—the First Lord and his naval counterpart, the First Sea Lord, and their staffs—had come to recognize the power to influence events thousands of miles away which the cable and wireless offered to them. Strategical as well as tactical control was now theirs. They were entranced by the prospect of moving fleets and squadrons and even individual men-of-war about the oceans of the world: and then matching their cabled orders by shifting miniature replicas on the huge map in the War Room at the Admiralty. The new sense of power was intoxicating, and no one relished it with greater satisfaction than Winston Churchill, First Lord of the Admiralty—a young man with an unsurpassed spirit and zest for war, and with a keen but still unmatured knowledge of its art and practice. Churchill had been at the Admiralty since 1911. He had seen his First Sea Lords come and go while he added, year by year, and with prodigious speed, to his comprehension of the meaning and facts of maritime power. He was a civil leader, with responsibility to the Cabinet, of the greatest single fighting force in the world—a fleet of hundreds of men-of-war scattered over the globe on whom the survival of Britain and her Empire entirely rested. Already Churchill's knowledge of the navy— from the penetrating power of a 15-inch armour-piercing shell against Krupp armour plate at 12,000 yards to the coal consumption of a light cruiser—was more comprehensive than that of many serving officers. His self-confidence and his self-assertiveness had multiplied with his growing knowledge and the growing imminence of war. In Britain in August 1914 there was no one more eager for combat; and no one more sustained by a heady sense of power. As First Sea Lord he had a steady, loyal 60-year-old admiral of royal blood, beloved and respected by the navy and the nation. Admiral Prince Louis of Battenberg, who married his cousin, a grand-daughter of Queen Victoria, and was the father of the present Lord Louis Mountbatten, would have gone far—but perhaps not as far as this—without royal patronage. Prince Louis was a happy choice as a partner to Winston Churchill. Few other admirals would have yielded so meekly to the loss of their power. nor been so willing to rubber-stamp military decisions of a far-reaching nature far beyond the political responsibilities of the First Lord's duties. ('I concur' at the foot of memoranda became almost a part of the Battenberg signature.) Churchill appeared to think of everything and gave the impression that he had made provision for every contingency. After appointing two perfectly capable admirals to the Australia and China stations, who had made all arrangements for co-ordinating their plans to hunt down and destroy von Spee when war came, the Admiralty (and that meant Winston Churchill) then proceeded to move about the Pacific, like chessmen in a game played on hunches and suppositions, these two admirals, and the vessels of their squadrons. The absence in London of any war plans for the Pacific theatre or for the capture of the German colonies, the uncertainty of Japan's attitude, the ignorance surrounding the whereabouts of the enemy, all led to ever-increasing confusion in the hunt for von Spee. What the German admiral and his staff saw as a neatly closing trap of steel on three sides was in fact a mainly bewildered scattering of men-of-war of six different navies, those of Britain, France, Russia, Japan, Australia and New Zealand. Very few of them knew where their friends, let alone their enemies, were. No one, not even the French Government, knew where the French flagship *Montcalm* had got to when war began. The French admiral was supposed to put himself under British orders but he did not know this. The Russians were very elusive, too; not that their aged cruisers were going to be of much help. But the one ship which, by both British and German calculations, could blow all von Spee's squadron out of the water, was wandering about the coast of New Guinea. Patey with the *Australia* was confident that von Spee was going to make for the Bismarck Archipelago. Before he could satisfy himself on this, he was told that a party of New Zealand soldiers was off to capture Samoa and that he must go and escort them. No sooner had he accomplished this task than he was sent off again back to New Guinea on a similar errand, this time to protect Australian soldiers bent on their own invasion. Neither of these expeditions had been planned before the war and poor Patey had been told nothing of them by the Admiralty until he was ordered to take his great battle cruiser to help them.

Far to the north, Admiral Jerram was having an equally difficult time. He had made plans for the destruction of von Spee's squadron which had been approved by the Admiralty in London eight months before war broke out. These included concentrating his ships north of the Saddle Islands where he could hope both to protect Allied trade and to intercept the Germans as they came out of or approached their base at Tsingtau—'my correct strategical position' as this admiral described it. Churchill was not satisfied with this. He wanted Jerram at Hong Kong, and ordered him there. 'I was reluctant to do so,' said Jerram, and obeyed. He understood Churchill's reasoning and knew how false it was. Churchill wanted him to operate with the battleship *Triumph*, the one ship in China waters carrying heavier guns than the *Gneisenau* or *Scharnhorst*. On paper (and this was what Churchill relied on), the *Triumph* with her 10-inch guns was a formidable battleship. But she was terribly old and terribly slow and her guns were slow-firing and old-fashioned, and they had a shorter range than the German guns. Slow and obsolete, hastily mobilized and manned by a scratch crew (including a number of volunteer soldiers who had never been to sea in their lives), the *Triumph* in a hunt for von Spee's crack cruiser squadron could be nothing but a liability, a monstrous dragging anchor. No wonder one of the *Emden*'s officers commented: 'Happily, we had in the First Lord of the Admiralty, Churchill, an involuntary ally.'

Nor was this the end of Jerram's troubles. Not only was the *Emden* already beginning to make trouble in the Indian Ocean, but he had to despatch one of his best cruisers to the west coast of North America for fear that the third of von Spee's cruisers, the *Leipzig*, would attack British trade and perhaps also some very small and weak Allied men-of-war in that area. His last disappointment was over the Japanese. He had heard with delight and high hopes of Japan's imminent declaration of war against Germany. With the full weight of the Japanese navy behind him, he would beat his way across the Pacific with his squadrons like a party of armed warders searching a wood for a single escaped criminal. It would all be over in weeks. But things did not turn out like this. First of all, Japan deferred the date of her ultimatum about Tsingtau, and then made the expiry date a week hence. The delay was exasperating, for every hour that passed increased von Spee's chance of making good his get-away. When at last Japan became an ally, it was all too evident that she was not much interested in anything but Tsingtau, the German colony of Kiachau, and the minerals of Shantung. The deal that Japan offered to her European ally was so shamelessly self-interested that it was difficult to know how to reply to it. In brief, Japan demanded British help in the form of at least one battleship for the attack on Tsingtau: and in return she would provide Admiral Jerram with a pair of cruisers—modern ones, certainly, but still only two men-of-war from her great fleets, the rest of which would be busy at Tsingtau. This was a savage disappointment for Admiral Jerram. By the third week in August there was no longer any question of searching for and pursuing von Spee. Confused by the constantly changing situation and the orders and counter-orders which arrived from the Admiralty in London, he was at his wit's end to understand his priorities. Was he to watch Tsingtau in case von Spee decided to force his way back to his only Pacific base? Or help out his partner in the East Indies, Rear-Admiral Richard H. Peirse, who commanded a totally inadequate force to oppose von Spee if he decided to storm into the Indian Ocean and ravage British trade?

Admiral Patey, with his more powerful force, continued to sail about the south Pacific between Samoa and the Bismarck Archipelago, beset by equally confusing and conflicting commitments. Early in September, news of the first attacks against Indian Ocean shipping by the *Emden* was made known in New Zealand and Australia, where contingents of their soldiers were waiting to sail to Europe. Public opinion in these two countries was at once aroused. If they were to send the best of their young men half round the world to help in the defence of Britain in Europe, then it was the business of Britain (with her vast navy) to see that they were properly protected on their journey. Only the best of the warships in the Pacific would do to escort the best of the Empire's young men. And that included the *Australia*, the one man-of-war that could outpace and outgun the *Scharnhorst* and *Gneisenau*. Once again plans were changed. As von Spee sailed on south-east across the Pacific, still believing that the enemy was closing in on him from three sides, his hunters busied themselves with other and mainly harmless activities, the Japanese exercising their appetites on the richest prize left behind by the Germans at Tsingtau, the New Zealanders and Australians picking over the remaining morsels of the German Pacific Empire and from time to time cutting a German ocean cable.

For the present, then, von Spee and his ships and men were safe, though they did not know it. Churchill in London, on the other hand, could contemplate the position of the German admiral with satisfaction as 'a cut flower in a vase; fair to see, yet bound to die, and to die very soon...'. And it was true that for von Spee 'the process of getting coal was one of extraordinary difficulty and peril'. But by exercising his resourcefulness, doggedness and planning skill to the utmost, by sustaining the spirit of his commanders and men, and by using a blend of caution and courage unsurpassed in the history of raiding sea warfare since the days of John Paul Jones, Maximilian von Spee was to survive the crossing of the greatest ocean in the world and meet his enemy in good fighting spirit on the other side of it.

Never was the German East Asiatic Squadron more vulnerable than between Pagan in the Marianas and Eniwetok in the Marshall Islands. Like explorers at the outset of an expedition, their supply train was larger than it would ever be again. It was also a very mixed fleet, varying from innocent-looking luxury liners and big purposeful men-of-war to dirty tramp steamers and one pretty vessel, the *Longmore*, a collier that was 'more of a yacht than a cargo ship'. At first, von Spee attempted to keep his odd assortment in neat and regularly spaced columns. Like this, for a short time and in fine weather the fleet made an imposing impression while sailing in two parallel lines, the cruisers in the van, the smoke from dozens of funnels forming together in a great cloud which fell astern and drifted high into the sky as black evidence of their whereabouts for the searching enemy. But neither the helmsman nor the engine-room staff of small coastal merchantmen and colliers were trained to the same exacting standards as the navy. When the wind and sea got up and the skies turned dark again, one ship after another lost station and fell astern or out of line. The train at once lost its precarious dignity and, except for the warships themselves, became a motley scattering of vessels, like errant marching schoolboys beyond the control of their masters. The fleet's speed dropped far below the most economical ten knots of the big cruisers, resulting in higher coal consumption. The responsibilities and anxieties of the commander-in-chief increased further with the rising wind. On August 15th it began to blow a gale from the south. The smaller coasters, pitching and rolling from sight in the huge waves, soon fell farther out of their stations and almost beyond recall. Sternly the *Nürnberg* (herself smaller and suffering more severely than some of her charges) attempted to chivvy them back into line. The livestock carried in pens on the decks of several of the supply ships suffered worst of all, and the cries of distress of cattle and sheep and pigs as they were thrown about, breaking their bones, were awful to hear. Most of them had to be killed and thrown overboard. With some 5,000 miles of the Pacific Ocean still to cross before reaching South America, this squandering of their precious and perhaps irreplaceable resources—their food and their coal—was hard to bear.

The rigours of their long, lonely journey were making themselves felt. For the officers and men (all burning for action), to the dispiriting knowledge that every day's steaming took them further away from their enemy were added the physical hardships of sailing in heavy weather in men-of-war stripped of many of their comforts and for half the time in darkness. They faced their lot philosophically. 'It is difficult to occupy oneself as in the evening all the lights are turned out,' wrote Captain Maerker of the *Gneisenau*. 'We can have an emergency light, but the ports have to be closed and blacked out, so that the heat soon becomes unbearable. Then of course there is nothing to do but think, and that's bad. I can really appreciate now how lonely the commander-in-chief is.' Life for von Spee was indeed lonely, and tedious and burdensome too. But his letters home to his wife at this time (August 18th) reveal how he was sustained by his self-discipline and his patriotism. 'Of course our life is very monotonous,' he wrote. 'No lights burning and the night lasts fully twelve hours. . . . The great suffering that war brings in its wake is unimportant in relation to the fate of the world. There is no doubt that our people will fight bravely. . . . It is strange how unimportant I feel when I think of the aims of the war, and how little I personally value my life and how willingly I would give it in the service of the Fatherland.' Now that they had lost their regular peacetime cooks as well as their Chinese laundrymen, the food was 'not exactly good, but then we have to think of the army, they are much worse off'. He also reassured his wife about the health of their sons, as was his custom.

Count Heinrich in the *Gneisenau* was reasonably comfortable as well, but conditions in the *Nürnberg* for Count Otto were more rugged. 'Everything is wet and nothing stays in one place until it is bolted down,' reported von Schönberg, Heinrich's captain. 'The crew have not a dry stitch left on them, nor any dry clothes in their lockers. As the walls are now completely bare, the red lead drips down everywhere and ruins everything.'

The little *Longmore*, rolling some forty degrees, was in danger of capsizing as the gale reached its height, and for a time had to be escorted away to the south before rejoining the fleet. Then the gale eased, the rain stopped, the tropical sun broke through the clouds, burning the decks dry so that they steamed as if on fire. There remained only a few hours' sailing to Eniwetok atoll, and the train sought to improve its formation as if sailing to a fleet review instead of an almost uninhabited atoll. 'All we saw at first,' wrote one officer, 'was the green fringe of palms between the sky and the water; then the clean line of the sun-baked beach appeared. We did not catch a glimpse of the whole circlet until we were passing through the south channel.'

Too much time had been lost on the voyage from Pagan for there to be any thought of recreation and rest for the crews in this sun-baked paradise. As soon as the cruisers had anchored the colliers and supply ships came alongside, the storm-battered little *Longmore* on the starboard side of the *Gneisenau*. Preparations for coaling began without delay: word had reached the lower decks that the wireless room was constantly picking up signals in English between their hunters. The routine of coaling, with its curious blend of industry and theatricality, was a familiar enough one to all the officers and men. The only way to endure its rigours was to the accompaniment of as much laughter and noise as could be mustered for the occasion. Much of the noise was created by the donkey engines working the derricks and the recurrent sound of coal tumbling down the chutes into the bunkers. Accompanying these sounds were the cries and occasional bursts of song from the men. Then there was the band's music. The ship's band played patriotic marches and light music far above the tumult and coal dust on the ship's bridge. They were the privileged few whose work was clean. But coaling made great demands on their endurance, too. They were expected to play throughout the labours of their comrades with only the shortest pauses, even though their repertoire was limited. It was hot work up on the bridge, too.

The men had earlier mustered in their special coaling rig, which allowed them liberal self-expression. 'All the old clothes that could

59

not be used for any other purpose were brought out,' wrote one officer. 'The most comical figures appeared. An old dress suit was hunted out or a fantastic costume from the last baptism of the line. A hat without a crown, a stiff collar artistically curved, or the ribbon of some Order across the breast, completed the equipment. Most of these comical fellows were ingeniously rigged out, and they helped to put everyone in good humour, although they soon lost their gloss after work had started. This healthy, unsophisticated humour was maintained to the end.' Towards midday with the sun beating down vertically, working conditions became almost intolerable. It was not so bad for those working on deck; they at least received the benefit of the light breeze that blew across the lagoon. It was worst for those shovelling the coal in the bottom of the colliers' holds, and for the men trimming the cruisers' bunkers deep inside their steel shell where the dust was thickest and the temperature at its highest. 'Protected by glasses and with sponges thrust into their mouths, the stokers would then stow away the precious fuel into every corner of the bunkers until they were only just able to creep out of them on all fours; a sharp look-out must be kept to see that no one was buried under the coal. At all the loading places were stationed men who had made notes of the quantities coming on board, and every half-hour their totals were chalked on a large board or announced in a loud voice, to revive flagging spirits.'

After a full day's coaling on August 20th, all the men were in great need of a full night's rest. Many of the officers and men of the *Gneisenau* were to be deprived of this by the further activities of the *Longmore*, whose little hold was now almost empty of coal so that she lay high out of the water anchored close to the armoured cruiser. Soon after midnight the weather got up again. The rain came pouring down, and a vicious gust of wind caused the lightly-loaded collier to slip one of her anchors and swing round the bows of the warship. There was a jolt as the ships collided, and it was sharp enough to cause the two big steam pinnaces and a rowing pinnace made fast alongside the *Gneisenau* to break adrift with two men aboard. An officer pursued them in a cutter across the choppy lagoon. The darkness was complete for no searchlights could be used in this search in case they would be seen by the enemy. After this the momentum of incidents that night gained the pace of a comic opera, with hazardous overtones. A man fell overboard, a jollyboat packed with a precious cargo of soap broke loose from the *Gneisenau*, and there was a brave rescue. The *Nürnberg* sent aid in the form of a cutter, which was confused with one of the *Gneisenau*'s own lost boats. After the most strenuous efforts, all were recovered and brought back to the ship, except one of the steam pinnaces which had no one in her. At daybreak this lost vessel was seen far outside the lagoon and almost on the horizon. 'There she was,' said Commander Pochhammer, who had been in charge of the rescue efforts, 'bobbing up and down as if nothing was the matter with her, on the far horizon, very much at home in the midst of the Pacific Ocean. She would be caught up on the crest of a wave and as she descended into the trough, only her funnel would remain visible.'

The incidents of the night were not typical of the efficiency and discipline which usually governed the activities of von Spee's East Asiatic Squadron. But worrying incidents of one kind or another were inseparable from a long and difficult journey across the Pacific under wartime conditions, and even the most harmless of them must draw on the reserves of patience and equability of a fighting force burning for battle. Like any highly trained athlete before an important track event, for whom the minutes before the crack of the pistol are the worst ordeal, the store of nervous energy which sustained the fighting spirit of these seamen could not be replenished. Every worrying incident, every false alarm that the enemy was in sight (and there was another of these two nights later) scored its own groove; and the greater the responsibilities, the deeper it cut. For von Spee the strain was worst, and after only three weeks of war it was already beginning to tell. His 'thunderbolt' after the *Gneisenau*'s performance that night was a formidable one, and 'was transmitted by the Commander and passed downwards through the hierarchical scale'. Everyone accepted that it was deserved.

While the coaling of the cruisers was being completed, von Spee ordered a conference of his senior officers to be convened on board the armed liner *Prinz Eitel Friedrich*, which still boasted many peacetime cruising comforts and was clear of the coal dust of the cruisers. They enjoyed some two hours of complete relaxation over luncheon and several rubbers of bridge after. Then they got down to business. Von Spee elaborated his plans. They were simple in principle, yet immensely complicated in detail. The third of his light cruisers, the *Leipzig*, he believed to be still off the west coast of Mexico, probably approaching the Galapagos Islands. A fourth light cruiser, the *Dresden*, was believed to be preying on British trade off the east coast of South America. However successfully she was accomplishing her duties, the *Dresden* was certain soon to be hunted down by the numerous and powerful British forces in the Atlantic. Von Spee intended to bring about a rendezvous between his own force and these two warships at Easter Island, midway between Chile and Tahiti in the South Pacific. Their strength would then be highly formidable, all the men-of-war being fast and modern and manned by seasoned crews. No doubt the British navy would react violently to this affront against their Chilean trade. They must soon face combat. God willing, and if they survived, perhaps they would round Cape Horn and deliver similar blows to British trade off the River Plate, which was always packed with meat and grain ships bound for Europe. Here the prizes were heady in their riches. From then on? Well, who could tell? Perhaps, against all expectations and predictions, they could fight their way back home. . . .

This, in essence, was the outline of intention von Spee presented to his commanders. The problems of supply and communication were equally unpredictable and vastly more complicated. Von Spee proposed to resolve them in the following way. The *Nürnberg* was to be detached to Honolulu for coal and with despatches to be conveyed through the neutral cables of the United States to Berlin. These would inform the German naval staff of the East Asiatic Squadron's past and future movements, and contain orders for the *Nürnberg* and *Dresden* to join him. These despatches would also include instructions to German permanent naval agents on the west coasts of North and South America to buy up coal and provisions to be instantly ready for their arrival in South American waters towards the end of October. These same naval agents were to transmit by wireless the most accurate and up-to-date intelligence on the movements of enemy naval units hunting for them. Finally, one of the fleet's armed liners, the *Prinz Eitel Friedrich* and the auxiliary cruiser *Cormoran*, were to be despatched to Australasian waters as a diversion and to prey on enemy shipping.

Von Spee took his fleet to sea again on August 22nd, and as soon as they were clear of Eniwetok, the *Nürnberg* broke away to port and set sail on an easterly course for the Hawaiian islands. The arrival in wartime of a belligerent fighting ship in a neutral port is an event that has always created excitement, and often diplomatic difficulties as well. The neutrality laws are so complicated that they can be interpreted in a number of ways. A German warship was formally permitted one call lasting not more than 24 hours every three months at an American port, and to purchase enough coal to take her to the nearest German base. In this case, Captain von Schönberg calculated that he could fill his bunkers with 1,300 tons, enough to take him to Tsingtau, although that base, now besieged by the Japanese, could never really be his destination. While coaling was proceeding, he planned to spend his time with the German consul at Honolulu, Georg Rodiek, passing on the orders from von Spee. He expected no difficulties.

Early on the morning of September 1st, observers ashore at Honolulu saw 'a grim, grey-painted three-funnelled war vessel come up over the horizon in the direction of Barbers Point'. At 6.05 a.m. she fired a 21-gun courtesy salute and was answered by the fort. She was looking very war-like, stripped for action and flying only the quarantine flag. A delegation of federal officials of the public health service at once went out to meet her, and soon the word was about the town that she was German. She was the *Nürnberg*, which had called there for coal only six weeks earlier, and was now 'back from her secret cruise at sea', as the *Honolulu Star-Bulletin* headlined its story on its front page later that day. She was an old friend at this American island, at least in peacetime. With the health officers still aboard, the *Nürnberg* was directed to Pier 7, and proceeded slowly down the harbour wall and past the stern of the American armoured cruiser *South Dakota*, a contemporary of similar power and silhouette to the German cruiser's flagship. Was it by chance that the American ship's band happened to be tuning up at that early hour of the morning? And that the refrain which they broke into as the *Nürnberg* slipped by was *My Country 'tis of Thee*? 'As its patriotic strains floated over the water and were wafted to the little group of officers who lined the navigation bridge of the German cruiser,' a reporter observed, 'they at once recognized the melody as one much similar to the national anthem heard throughout the British empire.' To hear *God Save the King* at that moment was an embarrassment, even an affront. It was certainly an incident which suggested that there might be difficulties ahead.

Georg Rodiek came aboard before the ship was secured alongside the pier, and he had bad news for von Schönberg. There was to be no coal for the cruiser, as she had refuelled twice already at Honolulu in the past three months. Von Schönberg told Rodiek to take him at once to the office of the Commandant of the Naval Station, Rear-

Admiral Charles B. T. Moore. This was a direct breach of international law, von Schönberg protested to the Americans. The last call had been made in peacetime, and this was the first request for fuel since the declaration of war. Admiral Moore was unyielding, but he allowed von Schönberg to telephone the C-in-C of the American Pacific Fleet, Rear-Admiral Walter C. Cowles. Admiral Cowles was more accommodating. The Germans could have 750 tons, he said, enough to allow the cruiser mobility in case of pursuit and battle (Japanese and British warships of far greater power than the *Nürnberg* were said to be prowling off Honolulu), but only sufficient to get her a little more than half-way back to Tsingtau. This seemed to be an uneasy compromise, and 'a high army officer', one local newspaper reported, 'pointed out that the *Nürnberg* will not be coaling for the purpose of making a "home" port but for the sole object of "prowling" the high seas in an effort to interfere with the commerce of her enemies'.

The coaling wrangle was not yet over. Rodiek, with great skill, rapidly concluded a contract for the coal with the Inter-Island Steam Navigation Company and the crew of the *Nürnberg*, enthusiastically assisted by the idle German crews of the interned merchantmen *Setos* and *Pommern*, set to with a will. They were watched by an admiring crowd of local citizens. Then Admiral Moore stepped in again and sent a message to von Schönberg that he could have only 550 tons. Back to the admiral's office went the captain and Rodiek. There is no record of the second meeting which followed, but it was certainly a fiery one. Von Schönberg later told his commander-in-chief: 'Without doubt the American admiral's action was due partly to gross carelessness and partly to fear of Japan. In the end he allowed me 700 tons; according to International Law I might have shipped much more, but I had already lost too much time in bargaining; as it was, I felt that bargaining was beneath my dignity and I let the admiral feel this.'

The precious day was wearing on, and the alarmist reports were increasing hourly. The Japanese armoured cruiser *Idzumo* and the battle cruiser *Australia*, it was said, were waiting beyond the horizon to pounce and annihilate the *Nürnberg* with their great guns. Von Schönberg was a commander who matched up to the highest expectations of Kaiser Wilhelm. His courage was beyond doubt. But his duty now was clear, and he had among his officers his commander-in-chief's son. The cables must be sent to Berlin and to the

German agents in the United States, Peru and Chile and then he must get away as soon as he could, with what supplies he could lay his hands on. During that busy afternoon, while coal and provisions (and a thousand copies of the local newspapers for the squadron) were piled into the *Nürnberg*, von Schönberg passed over the despatches to Rodiek in the German consulate. To be cabled immediately to the Naval Staff in Berlin, by way of New York, was von Spee's general summary of his situation, which began: 'Yap (one of the German Pacific radio stations) has not been heard since August 12th, since when telegraphic communication has been suspended; I have received nothing but the news of Japan's demands. I intend to transfer activities to the eastward, to the Chilean coast . . . *Emden* was detached August 14th, with 5,000 tons of Shantung coal, to carry on cruiser warfare in the Indian Ocean . . . Australian squadron is apparently following us. . . .'

By 4.30 in the afternoon the *Nürnberg* had taken in all her permitted coal, and she was well supplied with fresh fruit, vegetables and meat. Fascinated dockyard spectators had watched large bins of potatoes, onions, cabbage and other vegetables being hoisted aboard and secured on deck, while fresh bananas, coconuts and pineapples were strung from her rails and rigging like tempting greengrocer's offerings. Live calves had been driven up the gangplank, followed by trolley-loads of bottled beer. It was evident that the men of the *Nürnberg* did not intend to die hungry or thirsty.

Early in the evening the rumours further multiplied until they dominated the conversation all over the town. The local Japanese fishermen, it was said, were laying nets to foul the *Nürnberg*'s propellers and to prevent any chance of her escaping from the British and Japanese guns waiting just beyond the three-mile limit. The German officers had all made their wills in turn at Consul Rodiek's office. An official statement put out by von Schönberg tended to enflame further the melodrama of the occasion. 'We know not what fate may await us in departing from the neutral zone at Honolulu and proceeding to sea,' it ran, 'but this is a time when every German on land and sea knows his duty and is prepared to do his best. We may be met by Japanese, British or other hostile war vessels for all we know, and while I realize that the press is anxious to cover the past as well as the future movements of this vessel, I must decline to make any statement regarding the *Nürnberg* or the cruise in the Pacific.'

E   65

Before darkness fell there were more excitements and more demonstrations of patriotism at Pier 7. Many of the stranded German merchant seamen were not content to help with the provisioning and refuelling of the cruiser. They were anxious to do their bit. Amid cheers from the local German colony, and, according to one reporter, 'facing what may prove to be complete annihilation and death, more than thirty loyal German subjects joined the colours of the Fatherland', and marched up the gangplank on to the cruiser's decks. The climax was reached at 9.20 p.m. Georg Rodiek (and what an eventful day this was for him!) came aboard to bid farewell to the officers, and lastly to von Schönberg. 'No matter what enemy we meet outside nor its strength,' were the commander's last words to the consul, 'the *Nürnberg* never will surrender. We are going to meet whatever comes, and I expect my little cruiser will be the coffin for me and my crew.' Rodiek strode gamely down the brow in the darkness, the last to leave. He was deeply moved. 'The departure of the *Nürnberg*,' he said later, 'was the greatest sight I have ever seen. They are going out to almost certain death—for the *Vaterland*. The Germans never surrender.'

Among the assembled Germans on the quay a chorus of cheers broke into the disciplined strains of *Wacht am Rhein* . . . With only her navigation lights burning, and without a pilot aboard (von Schönberg had refused the offer), the cruiser moved slowly away from the pier and past the fully-lit *South Dakota*. This time there was no doubt of the friendliness of the American sailors, who lined the rails and gave three cheers, which were warmly returned by the men of the *Nürnberg*, the cruiser 'increased her speed quickly after getting under way and in a few moments was swallowed up in the darkness'.

The citizens of Honolulu listened for the distant boom of gunfire that night. But no flashes lit the horizon. There was talk two days later (and it was reported in the newspapers) that the *Nürnberg* had met the *Australia*, that the first enemy salvo had carried away her masts, and that she had hoisted the white flag after her decks had been torn asunder. But there was no confirmation, and only the local Japanese believed it. Was this the last they would see of the German navy at Honolulu? Had all that excitement really happened in just one day?

Von Schönberg had arrived at Honolulu confident that his pursuers were still far behind. But even the hardiest fighting sailor could not remain unaffected by that tumultuous September 1st, when the air had been full of rumours and even confident assertions that the enemy's big guns were only a few miles away. The feeling of mixed relief and disappointment that once again they were not yet going to do battle was this time very strong. Von Schönberg knew that his men needed action; some form of violence to bring relief to the tension from which they were all suffering. Before joining his commander-in-chief, therefore, he decided to carry out a raid. Almost *en route* to Christmas Island where the rendezvous was to take place lay Fanning Island. Here there was a British wireless and cable station. Its destruction would provide the men with some excitement and it would also be militarily useful; although they would have to use guile and be swift if their arrival was not to be reported to the world.

The *Nürnberg* reconnoitred the little island by moonlight in the early hours of September 7th. At first light his radio operator picked up foreign sounds from his Telefunken receiver, and soon intercepted the message, 'Suspicious ship in sight.' As dawn broke, von Schönberg sent off a cutter with a fully armed party and flying the French flag. The ruse worked. Within a few minutes his operator picked up a further message. It was a reassuring one. 'The suspicious ship is a French cruiser,' it ran. Before the cutter touched the shore it hoisted the German flag in place of the tricolour.

An English wireless operator was standing on the beach, with five others, all drawn there by curiosity. Later he wrote home, '. . . armed men jumped ashore, guns were pointed at us and an officer said, "Hands up, you are my prisoners!" ' Within a few minutes the armed party had surrounded all the buildings and were at work with axes severing the cables and smashing the offices, the radio apparatus and the electric accumulators. 'At eight o'clock,' this same Englishman wrote, 'another boat arrived and asked for all buried instruments, guns and ammunition. We had to hand over nine or ten crates full of instruments, twenty old guns and 20,000 cartridges. What impressed us most was the speed with which the operation was carried out. It seemed to take only seconds before we were completely cut off. We felt uncomfortable, but they had been very friendly and terribly polite. "Would you be so kind as to pass me an axe?" they asked, for example, before they cut down the flagpole. "I am sorry, gentlemen, but this is the war." ' The Germans were away again in little more than two hours, feeling rejuvenated by the experience. It was to have a disturbing influence on the activities of the whole squadron.

The cruise of the *Scharnhorst* and *Gneisenau*, meanwhile, from Eniwetok had been an uneventful and mainly dispiriting experience. The sun had burned fiercely during the day, making the ships like ovens below, while life was equally intolerable on deck without their peacetime awnings. The monotony and discomforts had been broken only by the frequent back-breaking labour of coaling, reports that the enemy was drawing near, and false sightings of hostile warships. For men trained for years in a spirit of aggression and self-confidence in their power to destroy, this constant retreat and evasion, this skulking in obscure lagoons while the unpredictable ether of the Pacific brought to their ears reports of an enemy who might be 5,000 or only 50 miles distant, all made unreasonable demands on the nerves of von Spee's men. To have the *Nürnberg* back with them, to hear of her exploits, was an event that was keenly anticipated. 'On Sunday, September 6th, we kept a particularly sharp look-out to the north,' wrote Commander Pochhammer. 'Early in the afternoon, the news came from the crow's nest, "Smoke in sight". It rapidly increased in volume and came straight towards us. Slender masts revealed themselves. . . . It was the *Nürnberg*.' The entire fleet hove-to in mid-ocean. The *Nürnberg* lowered a boat, and von Schönberg was soon aboard his flagship with the news they had all been waiting for: news of his own activities, news from Tsingtau and from the fighting fronts in Europe.

Never was a bountiful messenger welcomed more gladly. Signals of goodwill flashed from every ship in the train. In the heat of the equatorial sun, boats put out and made their way swiftly to the cruiser for their ration of fresh fruit and meat, and above all, the precious newspapers—the first since they had left Tsingtau so many weeks ago when the world had still been at peace. 'In the west the battle is fierce,' read aloud those who could speak English, 'but going well for the German armies.' From the eastern front, the news was less specific, and there was anxiety among those whose homes were in East Prussia. The naval news was mixed. Three German cruisers had been sunk in battle in the North Sea (and many of them knew those who must have gone down in them), but the *Goeben* and *Breslau* had evaded the British in the Mediterranean and reached Turkey. And Turkey was showing herself increasingly sympathetic to the German cause. Would she soon come in on their side? Already the speculation and argument began among the groups of sailors before the newspapers were half read. Then with delighted surprise they read the names of their own ships. They were not forgotten. They were in the headlines. They were famous. The crowds gathered more tightly around the interpreters and laughter broke out. So the *Nürnberg* was sailing out of Honolulu to certain death! So the *Scharnhorst* and *Gneisenau* had already been defeated in battle, their wrecks towed into Hong Kong!

The renewal of a sense of belonging to the world, instead of drifting aimlessly and eternally upon its surface, could not have been more effectively accomplished. To this quick cure of their melancholy and boredom. their own laughter added the final reviving tonic. Spirits were high among the sailors talking and singing on deck before turning in that evening. But Maximilian von Spee had recognized the symptoms and the warning signs. There remained ahead many thousands of miles with little prospect now of any action: only coaling and gunnery practice and evolutions, and the regular shipboard routine, and more coaling. Meanwhile the weather would become progressively colder and less congenial, and there could be no more news from home for at least six weeks. In his quarters in the *Scharnhorst* von Spee talked over their situation with von Schönberg, who told his C-in-C of the splendid effect on his men of the raid on Fanning Island: even violence with an axe against inanimate objects had helped. Von Spee listened and read the newspapers his subordinate had brought with him. It was remarkable how much useful news they contained, not only of the war in Europe, but of the enemy's operations in the Pacific. For instance, here was the confirmation that the German colony of Samoa had been overrun. A large force of New Zealand troops, heavily escorted by warships, had made the attack. Probably the *Australia* herself had led the squadron, and perhaps she was still there. Surprised at dawn and at a severe disadvantage in Apia harbour, she would make a wonderful target—the greatest prize in the Pacific von Spee could hope for. If she had left, the harbour was most likely to be sheltering other warships and supply ships. Surely, here was the opportunity to strike usefully at the enemy, at last.

It was a measure of von Spee's anxiety for the morale and well-being of his men that on the afternoon of September 6th, after weeks of sailing east across the Pacific to escape from a superior enemy, he reached the decision to reverse his course. Suddenly they were to strike south-west for some 15,000 miles towards their most dangerous adversary, consuming precious coal and provisions, and perhaps ammunition too, and at the best delaying their arrival in South America where they had all agreed they could be most useful. The admiral called a conference of all ships' commanders and revealed his plans in detail. *Scharnhorst* and *Gneisenau* would sail alone to Samoa, and without the burden of a single collier. Much depended on speed and security. The fleet train, under the charge of the *Nürnberg*, was to rendezvous with them on or about September 24th. 'The *Australia* is to be attacked by torpedo, the other ships by gunfire at long range (about 10,000 yards),' ran von Spee's directive. 'In the absence of the *Australia*, the *Scharnhorst* and *Gneisenau* will advance towards the harbour from the north and north-east-by-east in order to prevent the escape of any of the shipping. . . .'

With their bunkers crammed full, and more reserve fuel stacked on deck, the two armoured cruisers disappeared towards the south-west on September 9th, crossing the equator on the following day. The island of Apia was approached on the night of September 13th–14th. In the wardroom of the *Gneisenau* betting ran rife. 'Some of us were certain that there would be an enemy fleet at Apia,' wrote Commander Pochhammer, 'others thought that the English would not be so foolish as to let themselves be caught in such a trap. . . . The majority thought it most likely that we should encounter two light cruisers detailed to support the troops ashore. There were others even unkind enough to say that the nest would be empty. I supported the former, less out of conviction than from a desire not to dampen the warlike enthusiasm which reigned in the wardroom.' The same speculation was raging in both men-of-war. On deck it was a clear, tropical night, lit by stars and a crescent moon. The men, washed and showered and in clean linen (an invariable precaution against infected wounds before battle) stood about expectantly, smoking and talking quietly. From the necks of each of them dangled their identity discs and their issue face masks to protect them from flash and poisonous shell fumes. As a shrewd precaution against premature discovery, von Spee had ordered that the last carefully preserved tons of their top quality Shantung coal should be burned during the dash toward the island. So now above them from the four funnels there streamed an unfamiliar light-coloured and pure cloud of smoke, which added further to the feeling of purpose and imminent combat.

The men were ordered to action stations, and the decks emptied. The first light of dawn was brushed against the eastern horizon. The ships were steaming in at full speed leaving long white wakes astern. Then a huge deep red sun climbed slowly out of the sea, casting low rays towards the white line of coral and the darker land ahead, dominated by the familiar silhouette of the mountain of Vaea. The details of the anchorage and the harbour beyond suddenly became clear, and the disappointment—spreading with the speed of a shell flash from the spotters with their big Zeiss binoculars down to the stokers below—was hard to bear. There was nothing, nothing at all, only an American schooner and a small sailing vessel, and the Union Jack flying arrogantly from the tall German mast.

What could they do but put over the helm and steam away? To shell the few brown tents near the shore from this range would only waste ammunition and probably damage German property and kill some of their compatriots. And to destroy the tall radio mast on the hill was beyond the capacity even of these skilful rangetakers and gunlayers. The only act of defiance that von Spee could order was the jamming of the radio which must soon spread to the world the news of his whereabouts. Later that day a white boat was spotted putting out from the shore and flying the German flag. In it were two German planters, refugees from the New Zealand invasion, who were brought aboard the flagship. They gave von Spee a full account of the attack. The most galling news of all was that the German Governor had been treated 'in a very unbecoming manner'.

The melancholy and desolate lava fields of the island of Upolu along whose shores they next sailed seemed to reflect the savage disappointment of every officer and man. Would they never meet the enemy, from whom they had retreated for so long and were now striving to engage in combat? No one was suffering more from frustration and a sense of failure than von Spee, and he was quick to recognize that the guns of his ships must at least once fire in anger if he was to reach his eventual destination off the South American coast with his men in fighting trim. He decided to divert again from his course *en route* to the rendezvous, this time south towards the French-owned Society Islands. They would find a target at Tahiti instead. That night the two ships steered briefly north-west until they heard the wireless at Apia (now beyond jamming range) report their false course, then east again. First they must re-stock their bunkers from one of the colliers which had been detached from the fleet train and ordered to the little French island of Bora Bora. Fresh provisions would be welcome too, to be acquired if possible without revealing their identity to the enemy. So the names of their ships were painted out, and only officers with fluent French were authorized to conduct negotiations.

On the morning of September 21st, the small European colony of another remote Pacific island were startled to witness the arrival of strange men-of-war. The chief of police at Bora Bora did not know what to make of his guests, but presumed they must be French and ordered out a boat to greet them. He was warmly received aboard the flagship by the officer of the watch, and was told in impeccable French that the admiral would be delighted to make his acquaintance. Von Spee was surrounded by a group of officers, all talking French volubly, and welcomed him aboard. 'I would like you to supply me with food—fruit and some fish if you have any. Of course I shall pay for it, in gold—English gold, that is the currency I have.'

The French police officer was pleased and flattered by his reception, and for his part presented von Spee with a bouquet of flowers. On his return to shore to organize the supplies, he even suggested that some of his natives might like to take out their canoes with presents of coconuts for the *matelots*. The sale had been completed (and it included suckling pigs, live oxen and eggs as well) before French suspicions were aroused. One of the natives, returning in his canoe, had been sharp-eyed enough to read through the paint the names on the sterns of the cruisers. *Scharnhorst* and *Gneisenau* were not French names, were they? The chief of police was dumbfounded, but quite helpless. There was nothing he could do to warn his countrymen or their allies of the imminent danger. He had no wireless, nor other means of communication with Tahiti. Many months passed before it was known that the German East Asiatic Squadron had called at Bora Bora.

At Tahiti the French were in fact ready for von Spee. News of the Germans' arrival at Samoa had reached London via New Zealand two days later. The British Admiralty had been deceived by von Spee's false scent, but the French colonial office had been warned of likely trouble anywhere in the South Pacific. The defending guns at Papeete were manned and loaded when the two cruisers appeared over the horizon early on the morning of September 22nd, and little white puffs sprouting from the hillsides warned the Germans that at last they were in action with the enemy. Nor was the shooting bad.

The *Dresden* (*above*) and *Scharnhorst* at anchor in Valparaiso harbour and surrounded by sightseeing boats (*Süddeutscher Verlag*)

7 HMS *Good Hope*, Admiral Cradock's flagship at Coronel (*Imperial War Museum*)

The *Nürnberg* triumphantly at anchor after sinking the *Monmouth* (*above*). And the fugitive from Coronel, the light cruiser *Glasgow* (*Süddeutscher Verlag* and *Imperial War Museum*)

9 The 'County' class armoured cruiser *Monmouth* (*Imperial War Museum*)

10 The *Scharnhorst*, filthy after her long voyage and the Battle of Coronel, at anchor off the Chilean coast (*Süddeutscher Verlag*)

The first salvoes straddled the *Scharnhorst*. Von Spee examined the scene through his binoculars. He had wanted stores and coal before combat, but he dared not risk damage to his ships. He could see that confusion reigned on the Papeete quays, and men were running for cover. There were a taxi and a cyclist hurrying into the town from the harbour. A great cloud of black smoke was already rising from the island's coal depot, signalling the end of his hopes of fuel. Angrily von Spee ordered fire to be opened on the French batteries. The big 8·2-inch guns swung round in their turrets, their barrels fingering upward in search of the range, hesitated, and almost before they had settled, blasted out the first salvoes. The shooting was sublime in its accuracy. The grey clouds, each with its momentary scarlet heart, sprang up around the gun emplacements—one, two, three, and a hit. It looked so easy. In two minutes not a gun remained to reply.

The *Scharnhorst* steamed closer inshore. Better targets came into view, a steamer flying an outsize tricolour, and one of their own kind at last, a French gunboat, the *Zélée*. She never had a chance to fire. With the same devastating efficiency, the cruiser's guns tore her open amid a fountain of waterspouts and she capsized and soon sank in the harbour. It was their first taste of blood and the savour was supremely satisfying. The trajectory was low and a few overshooting shells had torn into the town. One had blown up a car (driven, curiously, by a fleeing Japanese), another exploded deep in a copra store. It made a fine blaze, and as the ships steamed away the columns of smoke rising high over the island remained in sight like twin victory columns.

The East Asiatic Squadron was in need of worthier foes than outdated shore batteries and a 600-ton gunboat. But the exploit had in part fulfilled its purpose. They may have revealed to the enemy their position and their likely destination, but this, some mischance was certain to reveal before long. More important, for the first time the targets of their guns had been an enemy instead of a towed canvas screen, and by their faultless shooting they had proved their skill. Their self-confidence had been revived. The new meeting with the *Nürnberg* among the Marquesas Islands on September 26th was therefore as happy an event as the earlier one; and now they all had tales to tell. What was more, for the first time on the long cruise the men were allowed ashore. It completed their rehabilitation. The French island of Nuku Hiva was all that a tropical Pacific island should be, brilliant in its colours and scenic grandeur, voluptuous in its rich foliage and flavour. There were, too, fruits and livestock of all kinds in abundance. Soon the ships were loaded with provisions and the decks were as crowded as the Ark's with pigs and chickens, cows and oxen, all punctiliously paid for in gold to the natives. The white storekeepers in the villages also received payment in full from the enemy, for anything that smacked of looting was quite intolerable to von Spee and his officers. After three months, all the ships were now in sore need of replacements of such basic and mundane things as matches and soap and buckets, and naval cleanliness had caused all the brooms to lose their bristles. Parties were therefore despatched to other small islands in this obscure group (many of the inhabitants still had not heard of the war in Europe), and business suddenly became very brisk at a number of stores. Needles and linen, blue overalls for the engineers, some special treats for Christmas, and even a sewing machine were procured and paid for with cash or promissory notes.

The squadron's sojourn at the Marquesas was the longest in their odyssey, and it was not until the evening of October 2nd that all the preparations for their long journey ahead were completed. Two ships from the train, their holds now empty, were ordered north to Honolulu carrying reports of their progress for the German naval staff in Berlin and revised instructions to the agents in San Francisco and Valparaiso for the disposition and timing of supplies. The logistical arrangements were highly complicated and had been minutely worked out. The message for San Francisco asked for 20,000 tons of coal and enough provisions for 2,000 men for three months to be available in south Chile by the end of December. Their more immediate needs were to be transmitted to Valparaiso. Laden colliers must be ready by the third week of October to meet them at a rendezvous to be notified later. 'They should also embark plenty of fresh water,' ran von Spee's instructions, 'and provisions, newspapers, 100 oilskins, 12,000 sets of woollen underclothing, ten strong fenders, 1,500 kilos of carbonic acid and 300 litres of glycerine. . . .'

CHAPTER 4

Rendezvous at Easter Island

As they sailed out that night into the Pacific, 'the cloud-crowned mountains shining in the moonlight', there were few regrets. The break had done them all good; but they were fighting seamen at war, and the knowledge that now they were about their business in earnest was invigorating after the indulgences of tropical island living. Soon the changing temperature as they worked their way south, crossing the Tropic of Capricorn on October 9th, added further edge to their spirit. But best of all was unexpected and dramatic news of their enemy and their own consorts. One night, faintly but clearly over 3,000 miles of the ether, came the call sign of the *Dresden*, the raiding German cruiser which had already caused such destruction to allied trade in the Atlantic before following von Spee's instructions (transmitted from Honolulu) to join him in the South Pacific. So she had escaped her pursuers, had already rounded Cape Horn and was heading towards their rendez-vous at Easter Island. But the *Dresden* was not signalling her new C-in-C; she was speaking to the *Leipzig*. Had she, too, evaded her British and Japanese hunters? The wireless room in the *Scharnhorst* could pick up no reply, but the distances were still far beyond the normal range of a ship's wireless, even the efficient German Tele-funken sets; and perhaps *Dresden* was listening too. On the night of October 4th–5th atmospheric conditions were again exceptional. Again they heard *Dresden* tapping out and repeating her message to her sister ship. Von Spee decided to take the risk of revealing his position by breaking in; *Dresden* responded immediately. The reply brought with it comradely comfort out of keeping with the manner of its telling, the staccato code informing them in swift and business-like dots and dashes of the *Dresden*'s whereabouts. Their reinforce-ments had not only survived; they were less than a week's steaming away. 'My position is 31.25 south, 89.58 west' (between Valparaiso and Easter Island), reported the *Dresden*. 'I have contacted *Leipzig*. She left San Nicolas, Peru, October 4th, for Easter Island, after evading Japanese *Idzumo*.' There followed more news of the enemy, which told them that battle could not now be far away. Accepting that von Spee had now escaped from the British, Japanese, Australian and French forces in the eastern Pacific, the British Admiralty had despatched a new force to intercept him from the west. A battleship of the *Queen* class, the armoured cruisers *Good Hope* and *Monmouth*, the light cruiser *Glasgow* and the armed liner *Otranto* had all entered the Pacific after leaving Punta Arenas in southern Chile on a westerly course on September 28th. The German agents had evidently done their work well. To have such precise and early news of the strength and recent position of the enemy was far beyond what they could have hoped for. The *Dresden* was also able to give them the good news that she had with her a collier with 6,000 tons of coal, and the *Leipzig*, too, had her own satellite, the collier *Amasis*, with another 1,500 tons. By this time, the problems of coal supplies had developed into something of an obsession with the C-in-C. Again and again von Spee referred to 'the continuous worry about coal' in letters home to his wife. These 7,500 tons, and the proof of the efficiency so far of the German agents in America, did much to allay his fears that his fleet train might be caught stranded in mid-ocean by the new approaching enemy. It meant that he could now give his mind to his first duty, the preparations for battle.

It was possible (and this was confirmed by a further message from the *Dresden*) that the British squadron was also making for Easter Island. The *Dresden* was therefore warned to search cautiously before their own arrival: 'Torpedo the enemy if the opportunity occurs,' added von Spee. While the fleet train, sailing in choppy and ever-cooler seas, continued on its south-easterly course, von Spee and his staff made a close study of the *matériel* power of the enemy from the details in *Weyer's Annual*, the German equivalent of *Jane's Fighting Ships*. A statistical evaluation in terms of gunpower alone showed the British at a considerable advantage. The *Queen* class of battleship carried 12-inch guns, which fired 850-pound shells. Their own 8·2-inch shells weighed only 240 pounds. The armoured cruiser *Good Hope* also carried a pair of 9·2-inch guns, while the *Monmouth* mounted a heavy battery of fourteen 6-inch guns. These were their most formidable contenders, with a total weight of broadside of some 6,500 pounds against their own 3,500 pounds. And yet there were so many other considerations: the comparatively older age of the British squadron, the fact that many of their guns were mounted so low that they could not be worked in rough seas, and the slow speed of the battleship, which would allow the Germans to escape under adverse battle circumstances. Nor was it possible to judge the quality of the enemy's personnel. Were they newly commissioned ships with reservist crews? Or, like themselves, veterans who had worked together for months? Above all, what was the quality of their commander-in-chief? Even the shrewd and efficient German agents in Valparaiso could not tell them that. But each side held one great advantage. For their part, the British still held undisputed control of the rest of the world's oceans, and could call on new supplies, and reinforcements too, at any time from their bases. On the other hand, von Spee's new reinforcements gave him overwhelming preponderance in light scouting cruisers. Speed and good intelligence must count for much in the inevitable battle ahead. Yet, however the statistics were calculated—rate of fire against shell penetration, quality of armour plate against muzzle velocity, squadron maximum speed against the seagoing qualities of the opposing men-of-war—the battle when it came must surely be a closely-fought affair.

With the renewal of target practice over the following days, the crack of the guns seemed to sound a more purposeful note, and the men working the hand-operated breeches of the 5·9-inch weapons worked with a new enthusiasm and deftness. Easter Island was only two days sailing; if the British were not there they could not be far away.

The British were at Easter Island. But they were few in number and in no belligerent role. The Chilean island of Easter is little more than a collection of old volcanoes, seven miles across at its widest point and thirty-four miles in circumference. About the island are a number of hills, up to 1,700 feet high, pockmarked by inactive craters. Every point of the island is accessible and the bleak grey-brown volcanic ash landscape is unbroken by ravines or even trees. Closer to the shoreline the surface is composed of disintegrating sheets of lava. The only vegetation is a rough grass which sprouts up reluctantly between the segments of old lava. In 1914 it supported some 12,000 head of sheep and 2,000 cattle, tended by a handful of the 'canarkas', or local natives (a tribe as eruptive now as the lonely rock on which they lived once had been). The farm manager was

English, one Percy Edmonds. Once a year a Chilean sailing ship arrived to take away the wool crop and meat. For company, besides the unfriendly natives, Edmonds had only a French carpenter and his native wife, and a German tobacco planter. Then on March 29th a curious little party turned up from England. It consisted of a formidable and handsome woman, Mrs Scoresby Routledge, MA, enthusiastic geographer and geologist and, back home, a leading light in the suffragette movement: she had even made arrangements for *The Suffragette* and other similar journals to be forwarded to Valparaiso for her collection later; her husband; another geologist, Frederick Lowry-Corry; and Mr H. J. Gillam and Lieutenant D. R. Ritchie, Royal Navy, who had sailed their little 90-ton schooner all the way from England; and a cook. The purpose of this expedition was to study the extraordinary stone statues which had first been discovered by the Dutch Admiral Roggeveen as long before as 1722. They had made satisfactory progress both in their studies and excavations by early October, in spite of the hazards of native uprisings, and had no means of learning of the war in Europe.

When von Spee's fleet train appeared from the east, and the ships in turn entered the anchorage of Cook's Bay, Mrs Routledge was hard at work at Raraku at the other end of the island. The news did not take long to reach her. A sailing ship once or twice a year was the most they could expect off Mataveri, the collection of huts which was the island's capital. Suddenly there were no less than a dozen vessels at anchor, from great grey warships to dirty colliers. They were German, it was said. Mrs Routledge, ever industrious, was unimpressed, and made it clear that she had no intention of riding for four hours 'to gaze at the outside of German men-of-war'. What did concern her was that 'the officers would come over to Raraku, and being intelligent Germans, would photograph our excavations. We therefore turned to, and with our hands covered up our best things.' Being a methodical woman, she then settled down to write letters for the Germans to mail for her if they should be on their way to Valparaiso.

Meanwhile, Mataveri had become the scene of unaccustomed activity. The squadron's paymaster, Stabs-Zahlmeister Braun, came ashore and concluded a mutually advantageous deal with Edmonds, who still had no idea he was trading with his country's enemy: 50 oxen at 60 marks a head and 100 sheep at 13 marks.

For most of the men of the East Asiatic Squadron, Easter was a bleak, chill, rain-swept place after the warm delights of the Pacific archipelago, and they remembered it mainly for its discomforts, hazards and hard labour. Here they experienced the worst coaling of their long journey. They had coaled at sea in a Pacific swell. They had coaled in still lagoons. They had coaled at night by shaded lights and at dawn had been too tired even to wash off the caked black dust under the shower. At Easter they coaled direct from the colliers in the uncertain shelter of the Mataveri anchorage, and when the wind got up and the rising seas threatened to smash in the colliers' hulls against the armour-plated cruisers, they resorted to the ships' boats and the heart-breaking business of manual loading, ton by ton, basket by basket. When the wind swung to the north, the little bay became untenable. But there could be no pause in the dangerous work: already radio signals suggested that the enemy was drawing closer. The whole fleet put to sea and continued to coal under the lee of the southerly cliffs of the island. Rolling and pitching in the high seas, accidents were unavoidable even among these skilful and determined seamen. Ships' boats were damaged, and the hawsers of one of the colliers parted under the sudden strain of a great wave. Helplessly she swung past the stern of the *Nürnberg*, grazing her and twisting two blades of the cruiser's port screw. This was as damaging in its effect as a shell in one of her boilers, and repairs under these circumstances appeared impossible to accomplish. Yet somehow, with the cruiser heeled over at an angle of fifteen degrees in the open sea, von Schönberg succeeded in making some progress. 'We first tried hydraulic presses,' he reported, 'but they were useless. Then we constructed levers out of bars of steel. These were fixed in position against the bent surfaces and then pressed outward by levering with long screws, using the ship's side as a fulcrum, the opposite side of the bent surface being hit at the same time with heavy hammers.'

On their fourth day of painstaking and laborious coaling in the open sea, the wind swung to the south and forced them back into Mataveri Bay. Once again the half-empty colliers were lashed alongside, once again the men changed into their coaling kit; and to the canarkas ashore, when the sound of the donkey engines blending with the cries of the men came across the water, and the coal dust rose in black billows, it seemed that the white man's rites were no less elaborate and curious than those of their own ancestors.

There were lighter moments at Easter, and it did not rain all the time. There was, for instance, a lightening of spirits on the day the *Leipzig* arrived. Not only were there renewals of old friendships; for the admiral there was the welcome sight of no less than three accompanying colliers. Captain Haun of the *Leipzig* brought good news, too. The land fighting in France was going well, and the German Navy was having notable successes. A single submarine had sunk three British armoured cruisers in the North Sea in one morning. Far away on the other side of the Indian Ocean another British cruiser had been sunk by the *Königsberg*, the only other German warship still free, except of course the *Emden*. Everyone in the squadron who read of the *Emden*'s exploits in the newspapers brought from Peru by the *Leipzig* felt a sense of proprietary pride. Their little ex-consort had brought British sea communications in the Indian Ocean to a halt—no less. She had shelled the oil depot at Madras, setting it on fire. She had captured colliers to keep her own bunkers full and already sunk a number of enemy ships. Convoys of Indian troops sorely needed for the fighting fronts had been held up. Now it was easier to understand why their squadron had escaped unscathed from one side of the Pacific to the other. The depredations of the gallant *Emden* must have diverted their foes from the east to the west.

The *Leipzig* had carried out her own tasks well, too. She had instructed German merchantmen equipped with wireless to lie in the neutral harbours at Mollendo, Antofagasta, Valparaiso, Telcahuano, Coronel and Corral to intercept enemy wireless messages, and on hearing anything of importance to proceed outside the three-mile limit (so as not to infringe international law) and repeat them in pre-arranged code to von Spee. Less scrupulous arrangements had also been secretly made to intercept messages between official Peruvian and Chilean stations referring to the enemy's whereabouts and plans.

In spite of these elaborate intelligence precautions, there was one night of alarm at Easter. Fires were seen suddenly springing up from the island, their flames lighting the sky, their number corresponding to the number of the German warships anchored offshore. This was suspicious enough in itself. Had the English ashore heard, after all, of the war, and were they signalling some approaching enemy? At the same time, the *Scharnhorst*'s wireless picked up confused and unidentifiable radio signals. Von Spee decided that no risks should be taken, ordered the colliers to cast loose, and the whole squadron to proceed to sea. All that night, with their decks still covered in coal and the men at their stations, they patrolled round the island searching the horizon. Nothing was seen, there were no further wireless signals, and word from the shore told them that the fires came from burning grass, set alight to keep safely corralled for the night the livestock the paymaster had just bought from Edmonds.

The squadron returned at dawn to continue coaling. Precious time had been lost and precious fuel wasted. Von Spee angrily ordered the cattle and sheep to be slaughtered at once, and the ships' butchers, led by Stabs-Zahlmeister Braun, went ashore to carry out their bloody work. But it seemed that nothing could happen predictably and smoothly at Easter. The cattle which had already caused so much trouble ran amok at the sight of the knives. 'The more oxen were killed the wilder the rest of them became,' Braun wrote home to his son. 'Sometimes a lasso would break and the animals turned on the men. Then the butchers would drop their knives and run as fast as they could into the sea. . . . We laughed until we cried. When one of the oxen broke loose, a sailor was so scared he climbed inside one of the slaughtered animals. He looked ridiculous afterwards and had to bathe in the sea to get off the worst of the mess. . . .'

Besides Braun and his butchers, the only other member of the squadron who got ashore on Easter were the admiral and his elder son, Otto. Von Spee's interest in natural history could not be gratified on this barren old volcano, but his earnest curiosity led him inevitably to the famous statues, in spite of the driving rain. Mrs Routledge had no cause for alarm because there was not time for the long ride to Raraku, and father and son had to be content with the smaller exhibits. As the days passed Mrs Routledge could not continue to ignore the presence of this great fleet train, seemingly forever coaling off their shore, showing no lights at night, and on one occasion putting to sea in a most aggressive-seeming manner. The canarkas, she heard, were disgruntled because they were accustomed to being tossed some gifts even from the most humble passing schooner. But this lot were most unforthcoming: not a tin of food, nor clothes, nor any highly prized soap, from any of these great ships. 'On Friday rumours reached us that there was something mysterious going on,' Mrs Routledge recorded. 'Why did one officer say that "in two months Germany would be at the top of the tree"? We discussed the matter and passed it off as "bazaar talk".

On Sunday, however, news came from Mataveri that we could no longer wholly discredit. The German tobacco planter had been on board, and the crew had disobeyed orders and disclosed to their countryman the fact that there was a great European war. . . .' The details were hair-raising even to the most preoccupied geologists. England was about to be invaded. The Germans had raided the Thames and sunk eight or nine Dreadnoughts. The Kaiser was almost at Paris. The Asquith Government had fallen. England was now a republic. So were Canada and Australia. India was in flames. . . . The catalogue of terror knew no bounds.

'That Sunday evening,' continued Mrs Routledge, 'one of us saw the squadron going round in the dusk, the flagship leading. They had said they would come again, but they never did.' To all but Mrs Routledge the manner of the fleet train's departure was as shattering as its arrival. This phlegmatic geologist felt no need to justify her calmness. She was not that kind of a woman. Besides, it was all greatly exaggerated, as she was able to point out later when they found a couple of newspapers inadvertently left behind. Things were not so bad after all. The King and his Empire were both intact. The Germans were even retreating on one front. So she got on with her digging.

Once away from Easter with full bunkers, von Spee ordered intensified drill and battle practice, rangetaking and sub-calibre firing at towed targets. After three months of enforced idle cruising, they were going into battle. There seemed to be no doubt of this now. On their fourth night at sea they picked up a message from a Peruvian station reporting that the British cruisers *Monmouth* and *Glasgow* had been sighted off Valparaiso on October 16th. A message from German agents in San Francisco reported that a powerful mixed force—French, British and Japanese—was heading for the South American coast, and that their old enemy the *Australia* was on their heels again. Another Japanese squadron was reported near Hawaii. The East Asiatic Squadron might succumb to any of these in battle. But they made a swift and homogeneous squadron with tremendous *esprit de corps* and the best gunnery in the world. Their self-confidence at this time was marvellous. Von Spee knew that, and endeavoured in every way to sustain it. And so far their intelligence must be superior to anything the enemy could hope for. Von Spee ordered strict wireless silence among all but one of his ships to give the impression that she was alone. The British squadron off Chile were looking for him. Let them find him; but at a time and place of his own choosing. Given surprise and every tactical advantage, he had no doubt he could destroy this nearest pack of hunters.

There was a final battle conference between ships' commanders in the last hours before they left Easter. Off the Chilean coast in October, the weather would almost certainly be rough. Range was therefore to be kept to 7,000 to 8,000 yards, though greater if conditions permitted. Range to be closed later in action to increase the effect of their armour-piercing shell. . . . In the admiral's day cabin, von Spee, with his staff gathered around him and with the charts spread about the table, elaborated his plans to his captains. Was he showing signs of the great burden he had been carrying for so many weeks? Like his officers, he was tanned a healthy brown, and the furrows had for years been scored deep across his brow. Certainly neither his vitality nor authority had suffered. His instructions were precise and undeniably shrewd. There was an element of the magnificent about his tall figure and the clipped grey moustache and beard; and the timbre of his sharp orders, his gestures towards the charts, were all calculated to impress his audience. Here was the very personification of the successful naval commander fulfilling his allotted role.

Right up to the moment of confrontation with the enemy, the problems of supply haunted Admiral von Spee. But how magnificently the German agents were carrying out their delicate and demanding work! And what comfort and assurance he derived from the knowledge that they were not quite alone in this remote corner of a distant and hostile ocean! They picked up a promised collier from San Francisco, and reassuring news by radio from Valparaiso told of South American ports with deep-laden merchantmen ready to cast off and proceed to meet them wherever they were ordered. Others were on their way: the *Seydlitz* with 4,300 tons of coal and provisions for six weeks, the *San Sacramento* from San Francisco and due at Valparaiso with 7,000 tons more coal and another 1,000 tons of stores of all kinds. And there were many more. For the present their immediate future was secured. It was the Empress's birthday on October 22nd and in the cruisers' wardrooms some carefully husbanded crates of champagne were opened and toasts were drunk to Her Majesty and to victory for the Fatherland.

Their last anchorage before battle was Más Afuera in the Juan

Fernandez group, only one hundred miles from Más Atierra, which had been chosen by Daniel Defoe as Robinson Crusoe's refuge from Pacific storms some two hundred years earlier. Compared with the wonders of natural history discovered by this shipwrecked seaman, von Spee again found little to stir his enthusiasm here. The population of fur seals had long since been plundered by ruthless mariners from Chile, and there was no sign of the rare and once abundant Philippi's seal. The admiral had to be content with taking notes on the numerous sub-Antarctic and sub-tropical seabirds, and with bringing aboard some of the summer-flowering plants and shrubs. For all but a handful of the officers, there was no shore leave: only the endless and backbreaking business of coaling in the chill, damp air beneath the inhospitable cliffs of the island. 'Here,' wrote one officer, 'we spent several melancholy days in the shelter of this gigantic rock, which frowned upon the pigmy line of our ships and was the silent witness of our laborious activity.'

Three nights later on October 31st wireless messages from two of their most formidable adversaries were heard, at equal strength which indicated they were in company. Besides the call signs of the *Good Hope* and *Monmouth* there came across the air the following night a much louder signal from the *Glasgow*. That accounted for three of them. But where was the battleship? A signal from Chile indicated that a battleship with three funnels (but one of these was a dummy, said the sharp observer) had passed Punta Arenas on a westerly course on October 27th.

CHAPTER 5

The Neglected Admiral

The British force advancing up the west coast of South America to intercept and destroy the German East Asiatic Squadron was under the command of a courageous officer, Rear-Admiral Sir Christopher George Francis Maurice Cradock. He and von Spee were contemporaries and old friends, and their service careers had run on curiously parallel courses. 'Kit' Cradock was born a year later than Maximilian von Spee, on July 2, 1862, at Hartforth in Yorkshire, the fourth son (Maximilian was a fifth son) of Christopher Cradock and Georgina, the daughter of an army officer. He joined the Royal Navy as a cadet in 1875, and for the last twenty years of the old century became as heavily embroiled in the acquisition and defence of his country's colonies and outposts as von Spee. But there were always better opportunities for military action for British officers, with their vastly more widespread responsibilities and more rebellious natives, than for German officers. Besides, Cradock early showed a marked relish for combat; and at this period in British history those with determination and influence in high places could usually arrange to be on the scene when trouble was brewing. As he made his steady progress up the promotion ladder he found fighting on land in Africa, the Near East and the Far East. At 22 years he was on hazardous garrisoning duties with the naval brigade in Upper Egypt (Gordon was to die the following year in Khartoum). He saw more action in the Eastern Sudan Field Force in 1891, when he was ADC to the Governor-General. He was at the Battle of Tokar and at the occupation of Affafit and was awarded the appropriate campaign medals. Gallantry for 'Kit' Cradock was almost a reflex action. He revelled in it himself and loved to witness it in others. Out in China, where he met and shared in 'the Boxer troubles' with von Spee, he was in the vanguard at the storming by land of the Taku forts, and watched with delight the gallantry of his fellow officers on shipboard. 'Let me call to mind the goodly sight,' he wrote, 'of those two destroyers . . . slipping through the black rushing waters of the Peiho at the opening of that furious and distracting midnight bombardment of the Taku forts, bound to attack and capture the Chinese destroyers and arsenal, knowing naught of what was ahead of them, and caring less.' At Siku, Tientsin and the arsenal at Peiyang, Cradock was always 'in the thick of things'. Further medals including the German Royal Order of the Crown, Second Class, with Swords, soon emblazoned his uniform. British Royal attention was further attracted to him, too. He moved freely in court circles, was appointed a CB in 1902, a KCVO ten years later, and was made ADC to King Edward VII. Even in the more settled first decade of the new century he contrived to exercise his gallantry; and how more suitably than on a Royal occasion? He was already a holder of the Royal Humane Society's testimonial for leaping into the Mediterranean at night to save a midshipman, when in 1911, as a Rear-Admiral at Gibraltar, he was told that a P and O liner had gone aground near Cape Spartel. On board among the distinguished company were the Princess Royal and her family and the Duke of Fife. Cradock raced to the scene, got the Royal party into a cutter and succeeded in transporting them to the rugged shore. He could not prevent their being thrown out when the cutter was swamped; but all survived.

'Kit' Cradock, in the words of one of his contemporaries, 'fought hard and played hard and did not suffer fools gladly'. He was as fierce and formidable on the hunting field as on the field of battle: 'A first-class man to hounds who went straight at his fences.' A young midshipman out with the Quorn recalled how Cradock had shouted as he thundered past, 'Look where you're going, boy, and get that damned cow-hocked quadruped out of my way.' Later Cradock was appalled to see this same youngster refreshing himself from a flask of milk. Cradock whipped out his own flask. 'Drink up, drink up, snotty, don't peck at it,' he ordered. 'Do you good, like mother's milk—Cockburn '76.'

Cradock's loyalty to his King and country and to the service to which he had given his life (he never married) was characteristic of his time. In this respect there were hundreds more of his calibre in the army and navy. Yet he was much more than an aggressive and fearless extrovert, sustained by that special brand of British privileged class arrogance. He was sensitive to the feelings of his men, and of his superiors, too, as he was to reveal in the weeks leading up to his first real naval battle. And there are hints, amongst the memories of those who knew him, that he had a deep feeling, almost a sense of union, with the sea and the ships that sailed on it. He himself could write of them with a touch of poetry and dark drama. 'A heaving unsettled sea, and away over to the western horizon an angry yellow sun is setting clearly below a forbidding bank of the blackest of wind-charged clouds,' he wrote in a rather touching little book called *Whispers from the Fleet*. 'In the centre of the picture lies an immense solitary cruiser with a flag . . . at her masthead blowing out broad and clear from the first rude kiss given by the fast-rising breeze. Then away, from half the points of the compass, are seen the swift ships of a cruiser squadron all drawing in to join their flagship: some are close, others far distant and hull down, with nothing but their fitful smoke against the fast fading light to mark their whereabouts; but like wild ducks at evening flighting home to some well-known spot, so are they, with one desire, hurrying back at the behest of their mother-ship to gather round her for the night.' In these words he unconsciously revealed, too, an extraordinary prophetic sense. Or was it only by chance that he set so accurately the scene of his meeting in the South Pacific with his old German friend, Maximilian von Spee?

It is easy enough to allow Cradock's hot-headedness and bravery to embellish with gold the character of a simple seaman. He was nothing of the kind. But much deeper or much shallower intellectual powers would have stood him in good stead between the first days of war and the evening of November 1, 1914. He experienced repeated bad luck during those weeks, by contrast with the good fortune which had sustained him all through his life—the 'Cradock luck' as he referred to it light-heartedly. But other factors beside bad luck, and incompetence at the Admiralty in London, brought about the series of failures that occurred in his command before he met his foe. His most experienced captain, and an old admirer and friend, John Luce of the *Glasgow*, wrote, 'I had the feeling that Cradock had no clear plan or doctrine in his head, but was always inclined to act on the impulse of the moment.'

In spite of the similarity between the backgrounds, the service careers and many of their personal characteristics (even their stature and appearance were similar, though Cradock's beard was a touch fuller, his eyes blue but less fierce), there remained wide differences between Count Maximilian von Spee and Sir Christopher Cradock. There were many reasons for this, both historical and inherited.

Germany had been a disunited collection of independent States when von Spee was born, and the German Navy had not existed. He grew up in the full turmoil of his country's adolescent precocity. Yet Germany was beset by deep anxieties. Beneath the aggressive self-assurance of the Prussians, in spite of their victory over France in 1870-1, there lingered a sense of uneasiness. It was rarely recognized by the older European powers, yet paradoxically it added a great impetus to Germany's drive for the world's riches. In the Imperial German Navy (after all it had scarcely taken part in the Franco-Prussian War), this lack of self-confidence flourished more readily. No number of new battleships or ever-more-powerful guns provided by their great leader, von Tirpitz, could wholly eradicate it. What could the Germany Navy hope to achieve against the might of the British Navy? At sea the British had held almost undisputed power in the world since the Napoleonic Wars; their roll of victories was unsurpassed. The courage and skill of the Germans in the war at sea were later to be widely respected; until the very last months there was never any evidence of defeatism. But they always suffered from an inflated measure of respect for their foe. In peacetime this deep-rooted respect was warmly appreciated in the British Navy. At Portsmouth, Kiel and Tsingtau, the officers got on well together. There were many friendships like that between von Spee and Cradock.

The fighting philosophies of these two admirals closely matched those of the services they represented. As one sailed on eastward across the Pacific, and the other rounded the tip of South America and drove north in search of his foe, they were both making their way inexorably to a meeting that would demonstrate to the world the strengths and weaknesses of their fighting spirit and skill, as well as of their *matériel* power.

Admiral Cradock's misfortunes had begun within two days of the outbreak of the war. He was then Commander-in-Chief of the North American and West Indies station. This was a most comfortable and sought-after peacetime command. It was also considered to merit only a mixed force of mainly aged cruisers. Suddenly, in August 1914, he was faced with the responsibility of protecting the important North Atlantic shipping lanes out of New York and Halifax. If these communications should suffer any interference (and they included large troop convoys from Canada for the war in

France) the results for Britain could be catastrophic. But there did not seem to be much likelihood of that. The British Grand Fleet at Scapa Flow distantly barred the escape of individual German raiders from their home bases into the Atlantic; and if Germany wished to commit her whole fleet to a breakout attempt, then Admiral Sir John Jellicoe, its C-in-C, was ready. He and his officers were 'longing for a chance of a showdown' with the German Navy. On Cradock's own side of the Atlantic, his chief worries were the two German light cruisers, the *Karlsruhe* and *Dresden*, both of similar power to von Spee's light cruisers and the only German warships in the Atlantic. These warships and Cradock's had been working harmoniously together in protection of European residents and property in Mexico during the revolution. Cradock was on especially good terms with the German envoy in Mexico, Rear-Admiral Paul von Hintze. When the *Dresden* helped the family of the ex-President of Mexico to escape, and carried them to Jamaica, Cradock had offered the German his own cruisers to help protect German property. Admiral von Hintze sent Cradock a nice letter thanking him for 'the marked generosity which dictated this noble act'. This was only three weeks earlier, when Anglo-German relations were as cordial as at Tsingtau. Then on August 4th they learned that they were enemies, and there at once followed a spirited game of hide-and-seek among the West Indian islands. Cradock came within an ace of catching the *Karlsruhe* on August 6th. The German had stopped in mid-ocean and was engaged in trans-shipping some of her guns to arm a German liner when Cradock's flagship came over the horizon. The *Karlsruhe* made off at top speed (an exceptional 27 knots); Cradock called up the support of the cruiser *Bristol*, which chanced on the German in full moonlight, and actually got some shots in at her before again the German made good her escape. Early the next morning Cradock's flagship missed sighting the *Karlsruhe* by five minutes, and the two opponents passed one another in mid-ocean just out of sight.

For several days Cradock heard no more of the two German raiders, except a definite report from the Admiralty that the *Dresden* was off New York. She was, in fact, off the Amazon. Cradock turned south and renewed his search, missing them both again. This was no serious reflection on the British admiral: besides the misleading information London cabled him, the area he had to cover was immense, and his opponents were swift and commanded by canny captains. Nothing was heard of the *Karlsruhe* and *Dresden* for some time. But soon British merchantmen carrying valuable cargoes failed to arrive at their destination. This was a worrying business for Cradock whose scattering of slow old ships was quite inadequate. Moreover, another threat was making itself evident. The Admiralty informed him on September 14th that from the other side of the world two much more powerful opponents were probably making their way towards him. They might go through the Panama Canal, inconveniently opened just a month earlier, and create havoc in the West Indies or off New York. They might destroy British trade off the west coast of South America. Or they might round Cape Horn and pick off British meat and grain ships sailing from the River Plate. ' . . . Leave sufficient force to deal with *Dresden* and *Karlsruhe*,' the Admiralty ordered Cradock. 'Concentrate a squadron strong enough to meet *Scharnhorst* and *Gneisenau*, making Falkland Islands your coaling base. . . . As soon as you have superior force, search the Magellan Straits with squadron, being ready to return to cover the River Plate or, according to information, search north as far as Valparaiso. Break up German trade and destroy the German cruisers. . . .'

Events had already shown Cradock that his existing force was quite inadequate to deal with the light cruisers in the Atlantic; now he was to divide his warships and deal with von Spee's squadron as well. He wondered what sort of reinforcements for this formidable new task he could expect. Cradock was the last commander to plead inadequacy. But how was he expected to deal alone with all these German cruisers on both sides of South America? What had happened to all the Allied naval forces in the Pacific, which had so unfortunately allowed von Spee to slip through their fingers? Apart from the Grand Fleet itself, with its thirty-two battleships and battle cruisers, its vast number of cruisers and destroyers, there were enormous reserves of naval power to draw on in the Mediterranean and elsewhere. All that he was to receive in the way of reinforcements, he learnt, was an old battleship, and a modern armoured cruiser, the *Defence*. The first would provide him with the gun power for his task, but not the speed to hunt as well as destroy. The second would of course be most valuable. She was as powerful and as fast as one of von Spee's ships. But when would she arrive? Meanwhile the total strength of Cradock's force for the fearsome task ahead consisted of: his own old armoured cruiser the *Good*

Hope, only recently commissioned and with a raw crew which included a number of reservists, cadets, midshipmen and boys as young as fifteen; the smaller and equally old *Monmouth* also with a raw crew and only 6-inch guns ('with their wretched pea-shooters, they can neither fight nor run . . .' Admiral Fisher had written of this class of cruiser); a new, fast light cruiser, the *Glasgow*, as good as any von Spee had, but quite unfit to fight armoured ships; and a massive great white elephant, the ex-passenger liner *Otranto*. Cradock's men affectionately referred to her as the 'sardine tin'. She made a marvellous target for the most inexperienced gunlayer, had only a few light guns with which to fight back, and could not make more than 16 knots.

Cradock's misfortunes continued. The weather was appalling and delayed his coaling in the estuary of the River Plate on his way south. The *Dresden* could be found nowhere. Nor did his one bit of good luck provide any comfort. The *Karlsruhe* later blew herself up in an accident, but no one learned about this for months, and the anxiety and speculation about her continued. Then the false scent laid by his future foe, still far away in the Pacific, deprived him of one of the reinforcements he had been promised. When the report from Samoa on von Spee's call there added that the German squadron had sailed away on a *north-westerly* course, the Admiralty in London innocently assumed that he was not making for the west coast of South America. The German admiral, it was decided in London, must after all be making for Australian and Indian waters, in which case Cradock would not require the *Defence*. So the Admiralty cancelled that powerful ship's orders to join the *Good Hope* and *Monmouth*. Unfortunately, they forgot to tell Cradock. All the admiral was told was that von Spee was no longer an immediate threat, and he should now therefore attack German 'trade' off the Chilean coast instead. In fact there was no 'trading' taking place; the new German activity observed there by British agents was the more sinister one of loading colliers and supply ships in preparation for the arrival of von Spee.

Cradock doggedly continued south towards the tip of South America, and on the way picked up news which brought a moment of cheer and suggested that he might after all succeed in digging out one of his quarries. He met the British liner *Ortega*, which had just had an exciting time 'round the other side' of the Magellan Straits. A three-funnelled warship had fired on the liner and ordered her to stop. The valiant captain had decided to run for it, and by piling on every knot of speed and steering through narrow uncharted channels among the islands which abound on this part of the Chilean coast, had made good his escape. The German warship could only be the *Dresden*. So at last they had definite news of her. Cradock hurried on, pausing only at the little harbour of Punta Arenas halfway through the Straits of Magellan. There the British consul had more definite news for Cradock. The *Dresden* was almost certainly at a remote spot called Orange Bay. There would be supply ships with her; possibly even other light cruisers from von Spee's force in the Pacific. Their presence was quite illegal, of course; and it would also be against international law for Cradock to attack his enemy in Chilean territorial waters. He took no interest in such niceties.

Punta Arenas, like almost every Chilean and Peruvian port, was swarming with agents, from professional spies to observant and talkative port officials. Cradock took his squadron to sea at dead of night without lights. The problems of both weather and navigation were appalling. Gales blew unpredictably round the cliffs that towered above the narrow and uncharted channels. Mist and clouds obscured their course ahead, and snow storms intermittently blotted out visibility. They magnificently evaded all the hazards and got within striking distance of Orange Bay just before daybreak. 'The bay had several good exits, and it was necessary so far as possible to dispose the force so as to guard them all,' wrote Sir Julian Corbett of this episode. 'The ships were therefore made to close the place gradually from different directions, and then at the given signal each rushed in by a separate entrance. But not a thing was there. The bay was empty, not could the picket boat that was sent ashore find a trace of the enemy having been there.'

This was a further grievous disappointment for Cradock. Now failure had dogged him from Halifax in Canada to the very tip of South America. Nor could he see how he could immediately retrieve the situation. While intercepted wireless reports told him that the elusive *Dresden*, and perhaps another enemy unit, were off the coast of Peru, his own fuel supplies had fallen so low that he could not follow up the scent. There was nothing for it but to retrace his course and call for coal at the British base of Port Stanley in the Falkland Islands.

The sight of the Falklands was not calculated to bring cheer to the cold, wet and dispirited officers and men of the squadron. The two main islands, prosaically named East Falkland and West Falkland, together made a stark, grey rolling area of some 6,500 square miles. Only crofters from the more outlandish Scottish islands could feel at home in this isolated spot 300 miles from the Magellan Straits; and emigrant Scottish farmers formed at this time the majority of the 1,000 or so inhabitants. Sheep flourished on the tough grass. The approach to Port Stanley revealed no sign of a tree; only Government House, a cathedral, a scattering of huts, some basic dockside equipment and erections. The pubs were the one cheering sight. They were of direct British ancestry, with names like 'The Stanley Arms' and 'The Rose and Crown'. Better still, the beer they served was of an exceptional potency. It had to be to survive the long voyage through the tropics.

On this visit there was no opportunity to sample the beer or meet the local girls, who hurried into Port Stanley when the fleet was in. The ships arrived for the coal and nothing more, and as soon as bunkers were full Cradock was away again. Once again the situation had changed for the worse. Von Spee was, after all, sailing east across the Pacific. News of the German bombardment of Papeete had now reached the Admiralty in London, which cabled Cradock:

'It appears from information received that *Gneisenau* and *Scharnhorst* are working across to South America. *Dresden* may be scouting for them. You must be prepared to meet them in company. . . .'

Especially at this turbulent time of the year, cable and wireless messages were liable to serious delay and misreading. The news took two days to reach Cradock; and his own reply, much mutilated, was four days on the way to London. The intense cold, the grey skies and continuous high seas, the frustrations as well as the disappointments, were having their effect. His message home was anxious in tone and bore traces of asperity at the Admiralty's apparent neglect of his squadron:

'Without alarming [he signalled] respectfully suggest that, in event of the enemy's heavy cruisers and others concentrating west coast of South America, it is necessary to have a British force on each coast strong enough to bring them to action. . . .'

His failure to catch either the *Karlsruhe* or *Dresden* suggested to

Cradock that he could also miss von Spee's squadron entirely. The Germans might well slip through the Magellan Straits, just as the *Dresden* had done, destroy the British base at the Falklands, and create havoc with British trade off the Argentine, Brazil and even among the West Indian islands. This was a nightmarish prospect; worse by far than that of meeting the full might of the combined German squadron with his own pitiably inadequate force. So he told the Admiralty that he intended to take his own flagship back to his base at the Falklands, and await his promised reinforcements, and then concentrate his forces. The battleship, the *Canopus*, was on its plodding way. But what of that powerful armoured cruiser? He had heard nothing more of her. Cradock concluded his signal: ' . . . does *Defence* join my command?'

Nearly a week passed before Cradock received any reply to his inquiry. Meanwhile, he continued his industrious search among the multitude of islands and inlets, always suffering vile weather. A second search of Orange Bay had revealed an old sign, on which some careless German sailor had scribbled the name of his ship. It was the *Dresden*, followed by the dates on which she had hidden in this remote spot. The discovery further increased Cradock's depression. The very name of this elusive enemy ship was a taunting challenge. It was almost uncanny how his prey continued to escape him by a few hours or a few sea miles. Other intelligence that he picked up suggested strongly that von Spee was indeed fast approaching the South American coast, and that his heavy armoured ships were likely to be supported by no fewer than three fast light cruisers; perhaps a fourth if the *Karlsruhe* had evaded all his searches as successfully as the *Dresden*.

At last an Admiralty signal got through to him. It was dated October 14th and approved of Cradock's plan to concentrate his forces. It also told of a new British squadron being gathered together at Montevideo in case von Spee evaded, or destroyed, Cradock. This was of small comfort to Cradock, especially as among the ships this squadron was to receive was the *Defence*. She was on her way after all, but not for the support of Cradock, the commander deputed to seek out and destroy Maximilian von Spee. She was to go to the long stop.

Leaving the rest of his squadron with their colliers at an illegal coaling base set up among the deserted Chilean islands, Cradock returned to the Falklands to await his battleship. It was difficult to make a realistic judgment on the value of the *Canopus* which had been wished on to Admiral Cradock. Among the sophisticated armories of 1914 she should no longer have been called a battleship, a term which suggested the ultimate deterrent of her time. Any battleship built before the revolutionary *Dreadnought* of 1906 was obsolete. But she was still a battleship, and no cruiser commander (even as bold a sailor as von Spee) would put his ships against the 12-inch guns of a battleship. The *Canopus* might be capable of only some 17 knots, an inadequate speed to pursue von Spee; but with her in the squadron Cradock could at least feel confident of putting von Spee to flight, perhaps even of destroying him.

Cradock continued to be dogged by bad luck. The *Canopus* was due to arrive at the Falklands on October 15th but radioed that she was delayed by serious engine trouble. Cradock fretted at the delay, for every day brought new rumours of the proximity of von Spee to the Chilean coast. He was longing to be off to rejoin his other ships, and get at the enemy. He became increasingly irritable and difficult. He had never got on well with his flag-captain, Captain P. Francklin, whose approach to naval problems was more intellectual and up to date as a result of his years as an instructor at the War College. Francklin should have been his right-hand man. Instead, they took their meals alone in their own cabins and talked only when their duties obliged them to do so. During these days of increasing anxiety while he awaited his battleship, Cradock resorted to the company of the Governor of the Falkland Islands, Sir William Allardyce, a tall, upright senior civil servant, whose 'clean-shaven face, the rather judicial features and the thick black wavy hair proclaimed the administrator'. In Allardyce, Cradock could confide his worries and irritations. With the dog who was his constant companion at his heels, Cradock would come ashore every day and make his way up the slope of the hill to the Governor's residence, a two-floored stuccoed villa with a lean-to glasshouse along one side to catch the rare sun and protect the ground floor from the icy winter winds. There they would sit on each side of a big open fire, talking or playing chess. After dinner they might have a hundred up at billiards before Cradock returned to his ship. Sometimes the governor's ADC, T. N. Goddard, would be there, too; and on other evenings the two administrators might dine aboard the *Good Hope*. Goddard later recalled the bachelor simplicity of Cradock's cabin. The only decoration was a piece of old broken *cloisonné* porcelain.

Cradock once referred to it. 'I got it in China when I was a lieutenant and I have carried it with me ever since and it has always brought me luck,' he told them. 'But last month when we changed over into this ship from the *Suffolk* at half an hour's notice I only managed to get on board with my dog in one fist and this vase in the other. . . . I dropped this as soon as I got on to the *Good Hope* and knocked its head off, and I'm very much afraid that that means that I'm not going to see these Germans at all.'

According to another of Cradock's officers, the Admiral approached the Governor on a more delicate matter shortly before he left. 'There is just one thing I want you to do for me, Allardyce, if you would be so kind. . . .'

'Certainly, Admiral, if I can. What is it?'

'I shall not see you again. I will send my medals and decorations ashore to you for safe-keeping. If the Germans do come here and occupy these islands will you bury them? Then when the war is over I would be grateful if you would send them home to my people.' He passed the Governor a piece of paper. 'Here is my address.'

For the rest of the *Good Hope*'s company the days at the Falklands were filled with normal shipboard duties and a good deal of tedium. Especially in the evenings when the men were allowed ashore, there was much heavy drinking at 'The Rose and Crown'—'breaking it up and getting fresh with the girls' as the current slang had it. For the officers there was good shooting among the lonely bays of the islands, and sometimes they took some girls with them and had picnics by driftwood bonfires on the cold beaches.

On the last Sunday before they left, the *Good Hope*'s padre, the Reverend Arthur Pitt, came ashore and conducted the service in the little cathedral. It was packed with islanders and with the ship's company. The disparity in the age and appearance of the middle-aged reservists and the very young raw recruits was on this occasion especially noticeable. It was a poignant moment for the islanders in the congregation. A sheep farmer's daughter who was there that Sunday wrote to an officer friend in the *Glasgow*: 'The sermon was most touching and I was not the only one who wept: ". . . and after all it was Christ who made the supreme sacrifice [it ran] so that we who came after him might be saved. The time may be not far distant when we may be called upon to do the same and who are we to flinch from following Our Lord's example and laying down our lives so that our folks at home shall be saved from the domination of a ruthless foe. That reminds me," he continued, "only yesterday I had the glad tidings that my wife had presented me with a daughter, our first-born. I wonder if I shall ever see the bairn. . . ."

'After the service we all stood outside on the green chatting to the officers; the midshipmen and cadets in their Eton [round] jackets and gold buttons looked such children.'

The *Canopus* arrived at last on October 22nd, a week late. The great grey-painted 14,000-ton vessel steamed slowly in on a grey sea beneath a grey sky. Her silhouette might appear a trifle unfashionable, and her guns were certainly not of the most recent mark. But they were 12-inch guns, each 35 feet long, firing a shell more than three times the weight of von Spee's heaviest. She was a reassuring sight to all those who watched her come in between Charles Point and the Cape Pembroke lighthouse and drop anchor in Port William, close to the smaller, frailer *Good Hope*. Her captain reported at once to Cradock. They had had an unpleasant passage. They had been delayed by heavy seas as well as the troubles to her old reciprocating engines. These could not manage more than 12 knots, his engineer commander had told him, and would have to be overhauled before the ship could proceed. It would take about four days.

This was too much for Cradock. Twelve knots against von Spee's 22 knots! For a naval officer whose whole training had been shaped to lead him to a swift and decisive naval battle (the final justification and culmination of his life) the thought of meeting his foe while encumbered by a lumbering, half-crippled man-of-war was quite unacceptable. His whole instinct revolted against a defensive combat. Seven years before the war he had written: 'Putting rashness on one side as unforgiveable, I often think whether taking *any risk whatever* in these big and valuable ships of ours is justifiable. It is no crime to crawl about in your vessel, but if the Navy subsides into such ways in time of peace, where will the nerve be when war requires it. . . ?' 'Kit' Cradock had the nerve, no matter what the odds. He was a hunter, bent on the pursuit and the kill; whether with the Leicestershire Quorn or the South American Squadron of the Royal Navy. He rejected this white elephant out of hand. He would leave the battleship, with her 12-inch guns, behind. He would sail at once to rejoin his other cruisers. The *Canopus* could follow, escorting some colliers, when she was ready.

The *Good Hope* steamed out of Port Stanley, black smoke streaming from her four tall funnels, on the same day. She left behind a single member of her crew, a stoker who had been hurriedly recruited in the West Indies and had been recently arrested in a drunken brawl outside the 'Rose and Crown'. 'Half Stanley was on the little stone jetty to say good-bye,' one of the locals remembered, '. . . it was a grey, blustery morning. . . . It was with heavy hearts we drifted away to our homes.'

A few days later, the *Canopus*'s captain discovered that his engines were really in very good shape. The strain of imminent battle and the perils of the long journey had evidently proved too much for the mental stability of one engineer commander who had deliberately falsified his reports. The *Canopus*, it seemed, could manage $16\frac{1}{2}$ knots (the speed of the *Otranto*) without any difficulty. But by then Cradock was too far away. The unfortunate man was sent home under medical attention.

The preliminaries to the Battle of Coronel were accompanied, like some discordant and ever more excited chorus, by the clash and counter-clash of morse code above the bleak Chilean coastal waters. Every new message from the neutral wireless stations on shore, from the German and British agents who knew that their tasks were fast approaching a climax, and from the warships themselves blindly searching for their enemy, heightened in the staccato outpourings of dots and dashes the tension and sense of imminent doom. With every new message, from friend or foe, with the closing of the distance between their squadrons, von Spee and Cradock each made a new tactical study and assessment of the position of the other. Both admirals were equally deceived. Because among the Germans only the *Leipzig* identified herself by wireless, Cradock steaming north fifty miles off the Chilean coast imagined that he was closing in for the kill; his immediate quarry a single light cruiser. Similarly, only signals from the British light cruiser *Glasgow* were picked up at short range by von Spee. Soon definite information from on shore told von Spee that the *Glasgow*, the most lightly armed of Cradock's squadron, was anchored at Coronel. He steamed as rapidly and hopefully towards this small Chilean coaling port as Cradock steamed eagerly north 'to cut off and gobble up' his supposed single and weak opponent. The most modern aids of science, the most industrious and cunning efforts of practised agents, were accelerating the tempo and increasing the strain of the battle's preliminaries; they were also misinforming the two commanders so that when they were at last to confront one another, they found themselves more poorly served by their elaborate intelligence services than Lord Howard of Effingham awaiting the Spanish Armada three hundred and twenty-six years earlier.

The *Glasgow* had been sent in to Coronel to collect and despatch signals on behalf of Admiral Cradock; and also to buy four dozen oranges for him. The increasing strain and atrocious weather were disturbing his stomach, and as he told John Luce, the *Glasgow*'s captain, 'they're good for the guts, y'know'. Most of the *Good Hope*'s company of young boys or middle-aged men, unaccustomed to the rigours of this climate as they were to sea warfare, were in poor physical shape, too. Outside the sick bay at 8.30 every morning there was a queue waiting for treatment to boils, ulcers and constipation.

By November 1, 1914, Admiral Cradock, renowned in peacetime in social and service life alike for his masterful manner and blessed good fortune, had experienced three months of war. Almost every week of it had brought failure and disappointment. Nothing had happened on which he could look back with satisfaction. It was almost as if the fates which he had enjoyed for so long had turned on him when they were most needed to justify the royal favours, the medals, the promotions, the honours which had been granted to him in the soft days of peace. What was worse, it was becoming increasingly evident that there was a more tangible conspiracy against him among his old friends at the Admiralty in London. In the Atlantic he had been sent to catch new 27-knot cruisers with old 22-knot ships. With the imminent arrival of von Spee into his area he had been refused reinforcements, except for an old battleship with ailing engines. His determination to carry out the task and do his duty never faltered. His orders were clear-cut; they were to destroy von Spee. Even when he rejoined his squadron and he could survey again the inadequacies of his *matériel* his determination to attack never faltered. A defensive role was beyond consideration. All that he did in an attempt to strengthen his situation was to order the modern armoured cruiser of which he had been deprived to join him as quickly as possible. This was against previous Admiralty instructions, and when the news reached London, his order was at once countermanded. '*Defence* is to remain on East Coast . . .' began the last message Cradock received before going in to battle. This new denial was not calculated to warm the spirit of an admiral in distant waters bent on a hazardous mission against a fierce and well-equipped foe.

Off the south Chilean coast, the morning of November 1st was fine and clear after patches of local fog had dispersed. A strong south-easterly wind was blowing, and the seas were already high. The little *Glasgow*, unaware that von Spee had heard of his presence and was racing his whole squadron towards him, left the port of Coronel with the messages and the four dozen oranges for the Commander-in-Chief at 9 a.m. She rejoined her flagship just after noon. The sea was too rough to lower a boat, and the papers and fruit were transferred in a barricoe, or towed cask. Cradock's ships had been hearing increasingly powerful Telefunken radio signals, all identified as originating from the *Leipzig*. The admiral therefore issued orders to his ships to spread out in a line fifteen miles apart and steer north-east by east to comb the area and locate the German light cruiser, John Luce with the *Glasgow* nearest to the Chilean shore. The chill sun came out fitfully between the low scudding clouds, the wind rose until the *Glasgow*, lifting higher and plunging more deeply into the troughs, began to ship green seas over her forecastle deck.

The *Glasgow* was the first to sight the enemy. As she closed on the *Leipzig* the morse code had increased in volume until it half-deafened the telegraphist in the cruiser's wireless office: an hysterical clatter as if a pre-talkie movie pianist had lost control of the overture. Then there was a sudden silence in the auditorium, the curtains were swept aside, and there on the screen was the enemy. It was at 4.20 p.m. when a cry from the *Glasgow*'s lookout at the masthead gave the news. Every man with glasses on the bridge swung them to starboard. Surely this was the *Leipzig* at last. What other ship could it be in this lonely storm-tossed sea? Captain Luce ordered the helm over and as the *Glasgow* settled on a southerly course to close the enemy, the distant smudge of a hull beneath the pouring smoke assumed the familiar silhouette of a warship. But she was not alone. More smoke was staining the horizon. The *Glasgow* increased speed, and running now into the wind the cruiser's bows buried themselves even deeper into the Pacific rollers. Within a few minutes the distant shapes of three men-of-war stood out from the grey sea. Two were larger, each with four funnels. The third was smaller, with only three funnels. Instead of the *Leipzig* alone they were facing the full might of von Spee's East Asiatic Squadron, steering on an opposite almost parallel course to their own. The *Glasgow* at once signalled the momentous news to her Admiral, increased speed to 20 knots and made for her flagship. Cradock's prophetic vision of seven years before, written in the tranquillity of Edwardian peace, was fast being translated into reality. Already 'away over to the western horizon an angry yellow sun was setting clearly below a forbidding bank of the blackest of wind-charged clouds'. Already were 'seen the swift ships of a cruiser squadron all drawing in to join their flagship'.

In the *Glasgow* ' "General Quarters" was sounded off and everyone dashed to their action stations, laughing and joking at the prospect of coming to grips with the enemy at last', wrote one of this cruiser's officers. 'Forgotten were the past three months of frustration, hardship and hunger. "Now we'll show them," I said as I buckled my revolver round my waist.'

CHAPTER 6

'. . . the light of the bright world dies, With the dying sun.'

The sighting of the enemy had been simultaneous in both squadrons, and the response equally joyous. The sudden cry ' "The English are in sight" ran through the ship like a message of deliverance', wrote one of the *Gneisenau*'s officers. 'It seemed as if all our cares had vanished. The men raced up and down the gangways and across the decks wherever their duties called them. As if at play the men fed the guns with shells. . . . Powerful arms rammed the charges into the mouths of guns as if they were strengthening a fortress wall.'

Like his old friend who was still hull down over the horizon, Maximilian von Spee expected to find only a single enemy cruiser. But von Spee was not dismayed when the whole squadron hove into sight. The day of reckoning had to come, and the omens were good, on both the spiritual and *matériel* levels. This was All Saints' Day; and the English did not after all have their battleship with them. Von Spee knew his statistics well. He knew that he could outpace his enemy. He knew, too, that in a calm sea the weight of his broadside was almost double that of the English; that in rough weather (and the wind was now approaching gale force) the lower main deck guns could not be worked because of danger of flooding the ships; that his own more modern and better designed ships hardly suffered at all from this defect. Above all, he was buoyed up by the confidence in his men and their gunnery. They would not fail him now. Nor was the sharp edge of his eagerness for combat dulled by his familiarity with his foe. Von Spee knew, and had liked and admired, too many Royal Navy officers to be affected by the sight of the flag of his old friend Cradock streaming from the masthead of the British flagship. After all, the *Monmouth*, too, was an old peacetime friend. He had come to know the ship and her captain well out in China, when 'the English and Germans discussed with one another the chances of war between their nations, and wished one another the best of luck when the scrap came'. The scrap had nearly come during von Spee's early days on the station. The outbreak of the Second Balkan War had led to an acute crisis between the two countries. Von Spee had heard of it when lying off Chifu at the entrance to the Gulf of Pechili with his crack cruiser squadron. The *Monmouth* was, in effect, bottled up in the gulf, 'at the mercy of the German squadron'. But 'Count von Spee thought first of his English friend . . . in his elderly cruiser', and had sent a boat with a warning message. 'There may be nothing in the yarn. I have had many scares before,' von Spee had written. 'But it would be well if you got out of the Gulf. I should be sorry to have to sink you.' But the *Monmouth* had already got away, and from the security of her base, her captain had signalled back, 'My dear von Spee, Thank you very much. I am here. *J'y suis, J'y reste.* I shall expect you and your guns at breakfast tomorrow.' But all that had happened more than two years ago. They were now really at war. Nor was the *Monmouth* alone. There was to be boundless bravery, but no chivalry of this kind, in the fight that lay ahead.

Two hours and forty minutes passed between the moment of sighting and the opening of fire. This time was occupied with the inevitable preliminaries to a naval battle, when the two protagonists drew about them their scattered ships, formed them into line of battle, and jockeyed for position; just as Tromp and Nelson had done in the great days of sail. For this was to be 'a slogging match', as one of the survivors described it, with the two squadrons of fighting ships in line ahead, fighting it out salvo by salvo: a real gun battle, unimpeded by those new weapons of naval warfare, the torpedo and the mine. By 5.50 p.m. the British and German lines had been formed up, the *Good Hope* leading the *Monmouth*; and behind them the *Glasgow* ahead of the lumbering great *Otranto*— the little cruiser and the ex-luxury liner looking together (in spite of the ominous gravity of the occasion) like the fat man and the midget in a music hall act.

This was a well-performed evolution. The Germans appeared less skilful in gathering their ships for battle, and when their line was formed it appeared more ragged, and although the *Dresden* had appeared the *Nürnberg* was missing entirely. Where was she, and the admiral's elder son? Meanwhile, whatever the disparity in gun-power, it was four ships against four ships, the Germans forming up with the *Gneisenau* behind the flagship, and the garrulous *Leipzig* and the *Dresden* following behind. With the British advancing trimly from the north-west, the Germans from the north-east, it was becoming increasingly evident that Cradock could still gain a useful tactical advantage if he could bring his fire to bear while the low sun was behind him and blinding his foe. For perhaps half an hour his own position would be safe, that of his enemy highly dangerous. Then, when the sun dropped below the horizon, the advantage would be immediately reversed. Cradock's ships would be silhouetted sharply against the after-glow of the sunset, and he would see von Spee's ships (if he saw them at all) as dim darker shapes against a dark horizon. To accomplish this Cradock must force an action as soon as possible. All he required was superior speed; at this crucial juncture, speed was more valuable than an extra battery of heavy guns.

By six o'clock Cradock's sweating stokers had worked up the squadron to their maximum of 15 knots. Without leaving behind the *Otranto*, this was the most they could manage. They were now on a parallel southerly course to von Spee, whose four ships, trailing a vast cloud of black smoke, were clearly visible at a range of twelve miles; behind them the rugged Chilean coast topped by the more distant cloud-shrouded Andes. This speed was not enough either to cut ahead of von Spee or to force the enemy into gun range before the sun touched the horizon behind the British line. Flags fluttered from the *Good Hope*'s foremast. The order was to close the enemy, and the four ships turned four points together. It was a bold and gallant move which left no doubt that Cradock's determination to hold the initiative and attack had not wavered. He was still the undismayed pursuer, the attacker who had never considered the odds, whether they were Imperial Chinese infantry at the Taku forts or five-bar gates in Leicestershire. Proudly a signal went out to the battleship he had left 250 miles behind: 'I am going to attack the enemy,' he told the *Canopus*.

For Maximilian von Spee the preliminaries to combat exercised his nerves and self-restraint to an agonizing degree. The weather conditions for accurate gunnery were appalling. The big German cruisers were rolling from five to eight degrees, the waves were

The victor of Coronel comes ashore at Valparaiso. With von Spee are his Flag-Captain, von Schultz, the German Minister, von Erckert, and the Consul-General, Gumprecht
(*Süddeutscher Verlag*)

12 An enthusiastic reception for Admiral von Spee at Valparaiso, where he has difficulty in making his way through the square (*Imperial War Museum*)

Von Spee leaves Valparaiso after his brief and discomfiting visit. The *Scharnhorst*, *Gneisenau and Nürnberg* are in the background; the Chilean men-of-war *Esmeralda*, *O'Higgins* and *Blanco Encalada* closer inshore (*Süddeutscher Verlag*)

14 Admiral of the Fleet Lord Fisher of Kilverstone (*left*), and the man he sent to pursue von Spee, Admiral Doveton Sturdee (*National Portrait Gallery*, and *Imperial War Museum*)

breaking over the forecastle and the spray was clouding the lenses of the rangefinders and even penetrating into the conning tower. The light cruisers from time to time almost disappeared from sight, leaving only a tip of bow or stern and crazily tilted masts above the surface of the sea. In the *Leipzig* and *Dresden* even the best gun-layer or rangetaker could scarcely hope to get a range and bearing on an enemy in these conditions. This would be a battle between the heavy ships and their heavy guns on each broadside that were high enough above the sea to be worked: twelve modern 8·2-inch German guns, against two outmoded 9·2-inch British guns; six new 5·9-inch German guns, against ten old 6-inch British guns. The theoretical odds were overwhelmingly in favour of von Spee. But there would be only a desperately brief period, before the setting of the sun and the onset of darkness, when this theoretical advantage could be translated into reality. Here, then, was the supreme test of skill of the Kaiser Cup gun crews of the *Gneisenau*, and those of her flagship.

Through the armoured slits of the *Scharnhorst*'s conning tower von Spee could just discern the narrowing of the silhouette of each of his protagonists as they turned to port towards him, battle flags hoisted and clearly visible. He was not yet ready for them. There was an hour still to go before the low rays of the sun which inter-mittently broke out from between the storm clouds and blinded him, dimmed to the glow his gunlayers desired. Von Spee ordered a change of course, away from Cradock, and thwarting his attempt to close the range. And so for almost an hour, through intermittent blinding showers and contrasting intervals of slanting sun, the two squadrons pounded south through alien, storm-racked seas. Both were burning for action, but the more powerful was denying the other the opportunity to strike until the time was right. Only once was the agony of suspense briefly broken: at 6.20 Cradock made a last attempt to bring his foe within the range of his inadequate artillery. Again von Spee steered away, keeping himself tantalizingly beyond harm.

The earlier excitement among the German gun crews had dimi-nished and the prolonged tension was stretching the men's nerves. Commander Pochhammer, hastening to his post in the *Gneisenau*'s conning tower, 'cast another glance at the casemates where the initial jubilation had long since given place to a grim silence. The guns were loaded and ready to fire, the breeches were low as the range was still very great.' When the time came, the *Gneisenau*'s target would be the *Monmouth*. 'Not long since . . . we had fraternized with her officers at Hong Kong and, in all friendliness, drunk the health of our respective sovereigns at meals. Those were happy days. Now we were ready to celebrate again, but only when she had sunk beneath the waves. . . .'

The turgid sun was clear of cloud, filling the black wave troughs deeper at every minute. The men in both squadrons knew with certainty the timing of the holocaust. The base of the sun touched the horizon, and before its perfection of scarlet geometry was destroyed, the Germans were turning in for the kill. In the *Scharnhorst* and *Gneisenau*, men with clamped earphones were calling out the range with well-drilled precision. At seven o'clock it was 12,000 yards; and at the same moment the last segment of sun was impatiently clipped off by the horizon. At once the shapes of the British cruisers were etched deep black in awful clarity against the glow in the sky; the darkness fell over the *Scharnhorst* and *Gneisenau*, the *Dresden* and *Leipzig*. Two minutes past seven o'clock. The barrels of three of the flagship's big guns drew back in their recoil as if inhaling and simultaneously spat out a shaft of orange flame. Its centre was deep gold, and grey smoke followed it less hectically into the air. A few sharp eyes followed the flight of the spinning shells up in their trajectory. The stunning crack which shot through the ship was followed by seconds of silence. There was time for bets to be placed. . . .

From the reeling, water-swept decks of the *Glasgow* the enemy line was only intermittently visible when the cruiser rose up high and paused before plunging deep down again. How could any gunlayer hope to do better than drop his shells in the general vicinity of his target? It did not seem possible that the precise scientific calculations, practised so often in gun drill, could be applied under these fearful weather conditions. Then came the *Scharnhorst*'s opening shots, seen as three momentary flashes across seven miles of heaving waters. Seven miles, and the target was just seventy feet wide. The seconds passed. Three spouts of water rose high in the sea, perfectly grouped, some 500 yards short of the *Good Hope*. These were ranging shots. Ideal gunnery would next produce an 'over' the same distance beyond the target. This straddle would be followed by a dead hit. One short, one over, then a strike. This was how it was taught at gunnery school, and sometimes under ideal conditions achieved in battle practice. Muzzle flashes twinkled out again from the *Scharnhorst*. Again the exploding heavy shells sent up water spouts, neatly patterned and 500 yards beyond the *Good Hope*. The inevitability of what followed was appalling yet scarcely credible. Only the best shooting in the world could have achieved it. A shell from the third salvo struck the *Good Hope*'s forward 9·2-inch gun turret. A sheet of flame shot into the sky and died at once. With one shell von Spee had reduced by half Cradock's heavy guns, the only guns which could fire effectively at this range, and the dead gun's crew had never fired a shot.

To prove that ultimate perfection could be repeated, the *Gneisenau* followed the same diabolical pattern round the *Monmouth*: a salvo short, a salvo over, a hit on the forecastle (or it might have been two hits) which set it ablaze. More heavy salvoes followed in rapid and precise succession, three in each minute, and then four, surrounding the two big cruisers with a deluge of fountains and striking again and again into the armoured decks and sides. In solitary defiance, the *Good Hope*'s surviving heavy gun returned the fire, one round every fifty seconds, almost blindly through the screen of water at the distant dark shape of the *Scharnhorst*.

Captain Luce and his fellow officers in the *Glasgow*'s conning tower who had witnessed this first onslaught, saw the flagship turn towards the enemy and he ordered his own ship to follow. After only five minutes of combat it was evident that survival now was impossible. The most they could hope for was the opportunity to damage the enemy's ships, which had no repair facilities, and force them to consume irreplaceable ammunition, and so make them more vulnerable to those who must next face this terrifying marksmanship. An act of self-immolation, at a price, was all that was left to Cradock. Within a few minutes he had begun to achieve his purpose. The old 6-inch guns of the *Good Hope* and *Monmouth* opened fire at their maximum range. The inexperienced gunlayers had little enough to guide them. With every passing minute the hulls of the German cruisers blended more darkly into the dusk. Through the spray-streaked telescopes only the muzzle flashes rippling along the sides of the enemy were clearly visible, and the dull shudder of another enemy hit, the shriek of shell splinters, and the intermittent sharp crack of their own guns made concentration and accurate sighting almost impossible. But it cheered the unwounded men to be firing their guns and revived the spirit of the hundreds at their posts below decks. At least they were fighting, and even some hits were reported.

For a few minutes the *Monmouth*'s fire was rapid and well controlled. But she was doing no harm to the *Gneisenau*, who was now firing all her 5·9-inch as well as her 8·2-inch guns at an increasing rate. Again and again she hit the British cruiser, and with every new fire she ignited, her target became more clearly defined in the failing light. After twenty minutes of battle the *Monmouth*'s forecastle again burst into flames, and she yawed out of line and began to list. Another heavy armour-piercing shell tore into the *Monmouth*'s hull abreast of her third funnel and exploded close to the ammunition for the starboard 6-inch battery. This whole amidships section was torn asunder by the explosion and misshapen steel debris and corpses were swept upwards into the night on a yellow wave of flame. A few raw but stalwart gunners (they might have been aged seventeen or thirty-seven) were still loading the guns and getting off rounds. The *Monmouth* was not yet dead. But she had reached that stage when the inrush of water through gaping wounds temporarily quenched the lower fires, deceiving witnesses that she was holding her own.

The *Good Hope* stormed on alone towards her enemy, into the half-gale and the great waves, into the growing darkness and the ever-increasing hail of shell bursts. She was a blazing beacon, her dreadful internal fires showing yellow and red through open gunports and shell holes in her side. Sometimes a gun might have fired; or it might have been one more explosion of cordite or shell. Cradock and his flag-captain and most of his staff were now probably dead, within twenty minutes of the first salvo. But the *Good Hope* sailed on, a flaming, harmless wreck, yet still able to cause anxiety to von Spee. Was she about to fire her torpedoes? Or even attempt to ram the German flagship? Von Spee was taking no chances, and turned away, still firing.

The *Scharnhorst*'s spotting officer observed and reported in clinical detail the climax of the *Good Hope*'s destruction. '. . . the deck was hit between the second and third funnels, probably by an armour-piercing shell. It probably penetrated the deck on the port side and passed right through the ship as a huge column of fire, almost as high as the mast and sixty to ninety feet across, suddenly shot up the starboard side. The funnels stood out distinctly against the background of flame. The column of fire was dull red, getting paler towards the edges, and was interspersed with greenish sparks that shot up like rockets, masses of debris were hurled into the air. . . .'

The *Good Hope* passed through her last agonies without on-lookers: at least she was spared this. From the *Glasgow* she was seen, after her final convulsion, lying 'between the lines, a low black hull, gutted of her upperworks, and only lighted by a dull red glare which shortly disappeared'.

By 8 o'clock the *Good Hope* must have gone down, with all her 900 men and boys, her flag-captain and her admiral who had taken their meals alone, her chaplain who had never seen his baby, all the ship's pets and the admiral's beloved dog. Darkness had fallen and the surviving protagonists were groping about blindly in the dark. The only sources of light were the flashes of guns firing at other flashes, and the nearly full moon which appeared fitfully between the gathering night clouds; and these only added to the confusion and alarm. The *Glasgow*, which had been under fire from the *Leipzig* and *Dresden* since the beginning of the battle and had escaped almost unscathed, found that whenever she fired the attention of the two big German cruisers was concentrated on her as well. Captain Luce ordered the guns to cease fire. For a few minutes there was a lull in the slaughter. The Germans had nothing left to fire at and von Spee was keeping his distance for fear of a torpedo shot from the dying enemy.

The *Monmouth*'s fires were almost extinguished, and when the *Glasgow* came alongside the floating wreckage of the cruiser, John Luce could see in the intermittent half-light little groups of men on her upper decks, many of them wounded. They raised their arms in greeting when they saw the *Glasgow*, for the ships were old friends. A cheer came across the tossing water, and then a chorus of cheers—Hip, hip, hooray. Nothing could be done for them; they knew that.

Luce was able to flash a signal to the *Monmouth*'s captain by lamp enquiring after his condition.

'I want to get stern first to the sea. I am making water badly forward,' the *Monmouth*'s captain flashed back.

'Shape your course north-west, clear of the enemy. . . .'

At that moment 'the moon peeped out again for a few moments through the flying squall clouds', ran one account of this last stage in the Battle of Coronel, 'and, almost underneath it, in its silvery beam, *Glasgow* caught sight of the grey shapes of three enemy ships apparently heading towards them. To Captain Luce this could only mean that once more the hunt was in full cry. Immediately he flashed to the *Monmouth*, "the enemy is following us . . .".'

The next crucial minutes in the conning tower of the *Glasgow* have been described by a survivor. A gale was now blowing, and the little cruiser was being dangerously tossed about close to the ruined wreckage of the big *Monmouth*, and 'the enemy were still bearing down on us in line abreast'.

' "I cannot leave my admiral," said John Luce grimly. "We will attack with torpedoes."

'Number One (Commander Thompson) took out a cigarette and tapped the end on the case with maddening deliberation:

' "Well, sir," he said in his detached rather superior way, "you know what our 'mouldies' are. [They have] never run straight once this commission. Besides, there is no admiral to leave. What's more, it not only means the loss of another ship and four hundred men, but there'll be no one to tell the tale. *Canopus* will walk straight into them."

'He lit his cigarette.

'The Captain hesitated. "Tell *Monmouth* to make off as best she can. Hard a starboard, full ahead together. . . ." '

The *Otranto*, which had wisely broken out of line at the beginning of the gun duel, was already making her escape to the west as fast as she could go. With the departure of the *Glasgow* only the listing wreckage of the *Monmouth* with a few unwounded men still aboard her was left on the scene of battle. Clouds covered over the moon and von Spee never found his second victim. At 9 o'clock she was still afloat and even making a few knots' progress haltingly to the north. Her dying and her wounded were put out of their agony a few minutes later. Von Spee's last ship, the *Nürnberg*, which had been detached earlier in the day, and had been struggling through the high seas towards the sound and flashes of battle, had at last arrived. She could find neither friend nor foe and to von Schönberg's exasperation the battle appeared to be over. He pursued some smoke for a while, then lost it: perhaps it was the fleeing *Glasgow*. He turned back and a few minutes later a hull which he mistook for the *Dresden* loomed out of the darkness. Von Schönberg took the risk of using his searchlight. The pinpoint of light revealed a shattered listing hull, with steam and smoke pouring from her and the white ensign still floating in the wind above. He gave her time to surrender, and then opened fire at point-blank range, steaming slowly from end to end. There was nothing the *Monmouth* could do in reply for her few remaining guns could not be depressed low enough against the angle of her list. Otto von Spee witnessed the enemy's last death throes. 'To me it was dreadful to have to fire on the poor devil no longer able to defend herself,' he wrote home to his mother, 'but her flag was still flying.'

The *Nürnberg* made one more run, pouring in another deadly fusillade of 4·1-inch shells. The shattered steel ruin rolled slowly over showing its red underside and its keel and disappeared beneath the waves. Again, not a soul escaped. Seven-hundred men went to the bottom with her. Even if it had been possible to lower boats into these stormy seas, for the *Nürnberg* such a risk was unacceptable. The moon had suddenly revealed smoke to the south-east. Von Schönberg had no news of the battle nor of the whereabouts of friend or foe. Cautiously he made his way in the darkness towards the unknown vessels.

By 11 o'clock that night, von Spee's triumphant squadron had rejoined the flagship and then formed a patrol line to steer north up the Chilean coast searching for wreckage and for evidence that the *Good Hope* had been sunk. For the first time since the war began they were no longer hunted men. It was a curious and exhilarating sensation. For the present Maximilian von Spee was in undisputed command of the South Pacific. At dawn there was a little ceremony to celebrate the occasion, a replica in miniature of those splendid royal occasions off Wilhelmshaven when the Imperial German Navy did honour to Kaiser Wilhelm II. The sun was out, the sea was calm. The light cruisers closed on the flagship and formed a line with the *Gneisenau*. The *Scharnhorst* steamed along the length of the line at slow speed. From her halyards there streamed the signal, 'By the Grace of God a fine victory. My thanks and good wishes to the crews.' Von Spee's men cheered loudly as the *Scharnhorst* slipped past with von Spee in full dress uniform on the bridge, acknowledging the tributes with a salute.

The *Glasgow*'s survival and escape were regarded by her crew as a miracle. For more than an hour the *Dresden* and *Leipzig* had been firing at her. For ten minutes she had received the full attention of the *Gneisenau*'s prize gunnery—all 5·9-inch and 8·2-inch guns. A single blow from one of these big shells which had pulverized the *Monmouth* could have blown her apart. Not one of them struck her. In all she was hit five times by the German light cruisers, and of these three of the shells did not detonate, and only one caused minor damage. By contrast with the misfortunes of Cradock's two big ships, the *Glasgow* did seem to have been born with a charmed life. Only four of her company were slightly wounded. The worst casualties were among her parrots. Many of the men had bought these highly-coloured birds in Brazil to take home to their wives and girls. There were sixty in all. They had been tenderly cared for, taught to speak, and, when the ship approached the Antarctic, they had been given specially-made scarlet flannel jackets. When the enemy was sighted and action appeared inevitable, all but one of them had been released. During the gun duel and in the gale and high seas that swept over the little cruiser's decks, the parrots had flown about, confused and stunned by the din. They landed on funnel stays or on the edges of the boats whenever there was a brief lull. Two were seen to land on the barrel of a gun just before it was fired. They were among the many casualties. Only about ten survived.

While the *Glasgow* was fleeing in the darkness at first west and then south away from the scene of the battle her wireless operators were struggling to get a message of warning and a report through to the *Canopus*. It was for some time a hopeless task. The German *Telefunken* sets were transmitting a high-pitched wail like the scream of a thousand Valkyries to jam the *Glasgow*'s messages. The ship's junior sub-lieutenant, Harold Hickling, glanced astern and saw a terrible visual accompaniment to this hideous chorus. A distant searchlight flashed out and the sky was suddenly lit with a quick succession of flashes. He counted seventy-five of them. 'Utterly dispirited and sick at heart after such a crushing blow I went down to my cabin to snatch a few hours' sleep before going on watch. As I pulled the curtains aside I saw the door of Polly's cage was open and the cage empty. I had forgotten all about her in the excitement of sighting the enemy. . . . Poor bird, the concussion of the guns must have released the door and terrified she had flown out, found her way on deck and perished in the storm. But I was feeling too sorry for myself to waste much sympathy on a bird. I threw myself on to my bunk, wet clothes and all, and put my hand up to switch off the light.'

At that moment Hickling heard the familiar, distorted rendering of *It's a long way to Tipperary* which he had taught the bird. 'Polly was sitting on the overhead boot rack with her head on one side, her black beady eye looking down at me as much as to say, "What the hell *has* been going on?" '

CHAPTER 7

Celebrations Ashore

For the Germans, the victory off Coronel justified a few hours of relaxation. It also required to be politically exploited to the full. It was as important to impress the Chileans of German invincibility as it was to despatch to Berlin a full account of the events of the past twenty-four hours. It was another beautiful clear morning on November 3rd when the squadron approached the bay of Valparaiso. By international law, von Spee could take in only three ships at a time. He was naturally anxious to see his sons after the battle, and selected the *Gneisenau* and the little *Nürnberg* to accompany his flagship; his other two cruisers were ordered to guard his colliers and patrol in search of the *Glasgow* and *Otranto*.

It was a memorable occasion. The city had a strong German colony and there were the crews of many German merchantmen anxious to greet them and to celebrate. At ten o'clock they were approaching the wide harbour. 'With increasing clearness details could be distinguished on shore. Then an inquisitive Chilean torpedo boat put her nose round the angle of the proud rocks of Punta Caraumilla and disappeared, in order to report our approach. A small pilot steamer appeared and lay alongside the flagship. Shortly after eleven o'clock we anchored at the place assigned to us. The *Scharnhorst* fired a salute in honour of the Chilean national flag and afterwards saluted that of the Chilean admiral, who was in harbour with several ships.'

The news of their triumph spread rapidly. Groups of Germans from the town and enthusiastic German seamen gathered in groups on the quayside and waved and cheered when the officers came ashore. Chilean civilians, who had so recently warmly welcomed the *Monmouth* and *Glasgow*, also turned out in force to celebrate the German victory. For those on shore leave this was a stirring and even bewildering experience. It was the first time any of them had been in a city after three months of cruising the Pacific, with all its privations and rigours and boredom. The place was bustling with activity, and there was so much to see. There were the trams, clanging their bells, and the people leaping out of their way. There were the great buildings, the naval school, the steep streets leading to the high part of the city. And there were the shops, full of the most inviting goods of which they had so long been deprived. The shops had been quick to adjust their window decorations to the occasion and the fancies of their new patrons. The newsagents soon displayed copies of the first editions with reports of the great German victory. There were photographs of German warships and portraits of the Prince and Princess of Prussia, who had paid Valparaiso a Royal visit earlier in the year. One bookseller had enterprisingly decorated his window with a map of Europe and had traced out in pinflags the state of the Eastern and Western Fronts. The war seemed to be going well for Germany. Guides were eager to conduct the officers about the city. 'Our friendly guide took us into a real café,' wrote one officer, 'something to which we were quite unaccustomed, something long forgotten.' A few hours earlier they had been fighting their guns in the cold and the wet, and the darkness, and a storm had been raging. 'When should we have thought . . . that once more we should find ourselves . . . in a café, seated on cushions, listening to music and looking at pretty black-eyed women?'

Even among those who did not enjoy the privilege of shore leave at Valparaiso, there was joy and gratification at the victory. 'I am well and almost beside myself with happiness,' one of von Spee's sailors, Hans Stutterheim, wrote home. 'I hope we shall soon confront more of these English and then we'll repeat our success. "Dear old Fatherland, you may rest in peace, because we are fighting the war for you. . . ".' The admiral's sons, too, were proud of their father's success and their own part in the battle. Von Spee himself in a letter to his wife wrote, 'You can hardly imagine the joy which reigns among us.' Yet already by November 3rd, and in spite of receiving news that the *Good Hope* as well as the *Monmouth* had gone to the bottom, the sense of uneasiness and insecurity which he had experienced since the enemy had begun to close about him 6,000 miles away at Pagan was beginning to reassert itself. It had been a great fight. But in the long term, was not the inevitable consequence that the might of the British navy would bring overwhelming force to bear against him, that retribution would now be swift and fearful? Not even the destruction off Coronel the night before last could quite counteract his own instinctive fatalism and the long-held conviction of British naval prowess and superiority. While at Valparaiso he was to confide in an old friend there, a retired naval doctor, 'I am quite homeless. I cannot reach Germany; we possess no other secure harbour; I must plough the seas of the world doing as much mischief as I can, till my ammunition is exhausted, or till a foe far superior in power succeeds in catching me.'

The insecurity of his position was confirmed within minutes of his arrival. Everything—his reception, the news he would receive, his own response to it, were all predictable. First the German Minister, von Eckert, and the Consul-General, Herr Gumprecht, came aboard the *Scharnhorst*. On hearing of the victory from von Spee, they were overcome with delight and heaped praise and patriotic clichés upon him. There must be a special reception, a banquet, ceremonies, speeches. Von Spee demurred. He wanted no ceremonies. He must send his despatches, take on provisions, and be away again in twenty-four hours. That was the law. Under pressure, he agreed to a modest dinner at the German club. But there must be no speeches, and it must be a brief feast.

Then von Spee became practical, and the result of his enquiries was all that he had feared. The British were protesting at his presence and were bringing all diplomatic and commercial pressure to bear on the Chilean authorities. A German cheque had been presented in Valparaiso on account of live and dead stock recently purchased at Easter Island, a Chilean possession. The British were claiming that it was against international law for the Germans to provision again in a Chilean port for another three months. They were also attempting to persuade the Chileans that it was illegal for German colliers to sail from Chilean ports to nourish Britain's enemies. And of course, for Chile, Britain's trade was vital for her economy; without it the country would soon be bankrupt. The military intelligence which von Eckert passed to von Spee was no more comforting. Tsingtau was under fierce siege by the Japanese, and there was news of strong Japanese naval reinforcements crossing the Pacific and working south towards the coast of Chile in search of him. Admiral Patey in the *Australia* was also reported to be moving east again. Nor was there much comfort from home. A telegram from Berlin told him that in the Atlantic 'all trade routes are strongly patrolled', and recommended only that all raiding cruisers should 'break through for home in groups'. Evading the day and night patrols of the Grand Fleet? Slipping up the English Channel, the most closely guarded strip of water in the world? The idea was ridiculous of course.

Meanwhile there was business to conduct ashore, and the duty call at the German club. On the quayside as he climbed the steps from his pinnace in his tricorne hat and heavily epauletted greatcoat groups of Germans and Chileans cheered him, and 'cameras clicked everywhere', he told his wife.

The dinner at the German club was a painful business. Like all voluntary or enforced *emigrés* abroad in times of strife, the members were especially patriotic and enthusiastic in their demonstrations of loyalty. Von Spee took the seat of honour with his two sons, his senior officers and his staff about him. One of the officers had thought it suitable to bring a trophy of the battle for the club in recognition of their hospitality. It was a saucepan from the galley, riddled with small splinter holes and decorated with a hat band 'SMS *Scharnhorst*'. It was, said the officer, the only object which the English had succeeded in damaging: a minor misstatement as the flagship had suffered other superficial damage from one or two hits. Then came the toasts. They were inevitably of a patriotic nature and von Spee and his party responded to them in proper style. Then one more intoxicated and enthusiastic club member rose to his feet. 'To the damnation of the British navy!' was his loudly proclaimed toast. This was too much for von Spee. He stood and raised his glass to his old friend. 'I drink to the memory of a gallant and honourable foe,' he said sharply; 'and without waiting for support or even compliance drained the glass, threw it on one side, picked up his cocked hat and made for the door—brushing aside the awed and silenced civilians.'

All von Spee's party arrived back on board loaded with gifts, from bunches of roses to baskets of early Chilean strawberries. Von Spee himself received his last bouquet on the quayside before he descended to his pinnace. A woman held out for him a bunch of flowers. He saw that they were arum lilies, and this seemed appropriate to the occasion and his own mood. 'Thank you,' he said to her. 'They will do very nicely for my grave.'

After the squadron left Valparaiso, von Spee took them briefly back to the remoteness of Más Afuera where they could be sure of privacy before a decision could be made on their future. Among the tasks which had to be performed here was the especially sad one of destroying the pretty little *Titania*. The supply ships and colliers of their train from which they drew their sustenance all acquired certain characteristics in the eyes of the men. (Some were steady plodders, some more unpredictable in their ways, others just comic.) When they left they were always sadly missed. The *Titania* was a special friend. She matched up so well to her name: so busy and quick and fairy-like in her ways as well as in her appearance. But now her holds were empty and von Spee decided that she was too frail to withstand the hardships of the turbulent weather they might soon have to face, and perhaps even of rounding the Horn. So, beneath the high cliffs of Más Afuera, explosive charges were placed against her side and the dainty little vessel which had served them so well for so long turned over and took her final plunge.

Soon after this melancholy episode they received news that another old friend had succumbed, too. This casualty was of a more serious nature. After sinking or capturing 68,000 tons of shipping in seventy days in the Indian Ocean, cleverly maintaining herself in coal and provisions from her captives, the *Emden* had been cornered and destroyed by the Australian cruiser *Sydney* in the Cocos Islands. Between them, the units of the East Asiatic Squadron had so far destroyed an enemy cruiser squadron and millions of pounds worth of shipping. Now there were five of them left. How much longer before they were hunted down and smashed as the *Sydney*'s guns had destroyed von Müller's *Emden*? The fall of Tsingtau after the long siege, announced at the same time as the loss of the *Emden*, helped to reduce further their post-victory elation. They had all known such happy days there. 'I am very sorry about the fall of Tsingtau,' young Count Heinrich wrote to his mother. 'I don't suppose the Japanese managed to get more than a heap of ruins, but it is a shame, such a marvellous place and so much work had been put into it, the beautiful parks, a second home for us out here.'

Spirits rose again with the arrival of later news from the fighting in Europe. Things were going well. And, better still, the German people had responded with enormous excitement and pleasure to the news of their own victory at Coronel. The Chilean newspapers were full of the delighted German reaction. These newspapers were delivered to them while they were anchored in St Quentin Bay in the Gulf of Penas, to coal, provision and restore their strength. The Gulf of Penas is about one thousand miles south of Valparaiso. It is a strange, wild and unearthly place. 'What a different prospect from the scenes which had hitherto met our gaze!' exclaimed one of the officers. 'We were surrounded by silent forests, rocks, mountains and glaciers. One of these giant glaciers stretched right down to the sea, and as the sun rose higher and shot its beams upon its gloomy bed, the glacier was illuminated and distinctly revealed its crevasses and moraines. It was a wonderful sight!'

Christmas was only five weeks away. Now that they had survived four months of war and had shattered the enemy, it seemed reasonable to suppose that they would still be together to celebrate Christmas in some remote corner of the Pacific or Atlantic oceans. So parties were sent ashore to gather decorative evergreen and to cut down numbers of the native pine trees: they were not quite authentic in stem or foliage, but a reasonable substitute for the real thing, and they promised to last well.

Von Spee and his son Otto again took advantage of the respite to go ashore together to study the natural history. It was a mainly unrewarding trip, but they both took careful notes of what they found. 'Low hills covered with mixed wood,' wrote Otto. 'Mainly juniper-type scrub, low fir and pine trees, birches, treelike heather and blueberries, the moss underneath knee-deep and creeping undergrowth. Often marshy.' They tried to climb a hill together, 'but the undergrowth was too thick to get anywhere in a few hours', his father wrote home to the Countess. 'The only living things I met were pretty little birds.'

Their sojourn was completed by the presentation of honours. It was a bizarre setting for such a ceremony, yet certainly appropriate and reassuring for all the officers, petty officers and men that they should be reminded again that they were not forgotten, however far from their families and the comforts of home they might be. News arrived that Kaiser Wilhelm had granted no fewer than three hundred iron crosses to the squadron, 1st Class for the admiral and 2nd Class for those who had particularly distinguished themselves. The distribution was to be made at the discretion of the commander-in-chief. The fair apportionment of these medals among nearly three thousand men was a difficult task. Von Spee awarded them first to his own staff, to the ships' commanders and certain gunnery officers, chief engineers and radio operators, all of whom had performed some exceptional service. He deputed the distribution of the others to his commanders, and ordered them to send their lists to him. On studying these, he was embarrassed to discover that both his sons' names were included; and Heinrich was only a very junior sub-lieutenant in the *Gneisenau*. In a letter to his wife, he confided in her his uneasiness, and told her how he called Captain Maerker of the *Gneisenau* and Captain von Schönberg of the *Nürnberg* to his ship to discuss the difficulty. Both commanders reassured their admiral of the complete objectivity which had governed their choice. Greatly relieved, von Spee had himself taken at once to the *Nürnberg*. Heinrich happened to be calling on his brother, and the father was able to give the good news personally to both his sons. 'It was very nice to see how happy they were,' he told his wife. 'Heinrich was especially glad as he had not thought it possible that he could qualify for an award.'

CHAPTER 8

The 'Greyhounds' are Unleashed

Forty-eight hours before the crushing British defeat at Coronel, formidable changes were made in the hierarchy of the Admiralty in London. They were brought about as a result of the stresses and passions and prejudices of the most fearful war in history. For generations the British had been brought up to believe that their navy was 'our sure shield', that when war came the Royal Navy would at once assert itself in some great new Battle of Trafalgar. Nothing of the kind had happened during the first three months of war with Germany. Apart from an early brush in the Heligoland Bight which had resulted in some slight German losses, the navy's record was one of a series of disappointments. The sinking of British warships by mine and torpedo had been much heavier than Germany's. In the Mediterranean a powerful German force had escaped through the English net and into the Black Sea, and had strongly influenced Turkey's decision to come in against Great Britain. On the High Seas (in the Atlantic, the Pacific and the Indian Ocean) German raiders were continuing to sink British merchantmen and successfully defying all efforts to hunt them down. Above all Admiral von Spee was still free and undiscovered. What was happening? No one could say. But the disillusionment among the British public was deep, and a target for their wrath had to be found. Talk in London's clubland and in the pubs all over the country began to acquire a sinister note. One name was mentioned repeatedly: Prince Louis of Battenberg. He had a German name and was the son of a German. He might be married to a granddaughter of the good Queen Victoria herself, and it was said he was a naturalized Englishman: but once a Hun always a Hun, that was what they were saying. There was talk of treason in high places, and what could be a higher place than the office of the First Sea Lord? The popular press took up the cry. Soon the chorus was so loud that the Prince could no longer disregard it. On October 28th he wrote to Winston Churchill that he had 'lately been driven to the painful conclusion that at this juncture my birth and parentage have the effect of impairing in some respects my usefulness . . .'. Churchill accepted his resignation with grave reluctance.

Where should the British now turn for a successor? Churchill favoured the return of the aged John Arbuthnot Fisher, Admiral of the Fleet Lord Fisher of Kilverstone. The enormous power and prestige of the Royal Navy in 1914 had been created almost single-handed by this extraordinary seaman, this 'living legend', 'this veritable dynamo', as Churchill called him. His years as an admiral had been dedicated, with dauntless zeal and industry, to the reformation of a service which in later Victorian years had grown senile, antiquated and reactionary in all its branches. Fisher's vast energy, combined with his driving ambition, his genius for gaining the ear and the support of kings, politicians and newspaper editors alike, his utter ruthlessness with those who sought to oppose him, had brought about a remarkable renaissance in British sea power. When he left office as First Sea Lord in 1910, the Royal Navy was the most efficient as well as the greatest in the world by a wide margin. He had made many enemies on the way, but the navy which went to war against Germany in 1914 was Fisher's navy. Churchill decided that Fisher, in spite of his seventy-four years, was the only man who could replace Prince Louis. He would stake his reputation on it; he would resign if he did not have him. Fisher 'used to come occasionally to the Admiralty, and I watched him narrowly to judge his physical strength and mental alertness', wrote Churchill. 'There seemed no doubt about either. On one occasion, when inveighing against someone whom he thought obstructive, he became so convulsed with fury that it seemed that every nerve and blood-vessel in his body would be ruptured. However, they stood the strain magnificently, and he left me with the impression of a terrible engine of mental and physical power burning and throbbing in that aged frame.'

Fisher was re-appointed First Sea Lord on October 30th. The moment he swept into the Admiralty, it was clear to everyone that there were going to be more changes among the senior staff. Fisher had always been a savage wielder of a new broom. Battenberg he regarded as 'a cypher and Winston's facile dupe!' His first target was Vice-Admiral Doveton Sturdee, Battenberg's Chief of Naval

Staff. Fisher would not entertain for one moment working with this officer, who years before had given the impression that he supported one of Fisher's bitterest enemies, Admiral Lord Charles Beresford. He would have to go. Look at the disposition of forces against Admiral von Spee! 'Never such rot as perpetrated by Sturdee in his world-wide dispersal of weak units!' he exclaimed in a letter to one of his admirals. 'I'm in the position of a chess player coming into a game after some d——d bad moves have been made in the opening of the game by a pedantic ass, which Sturdee is, has been, and always will be! It's very difficult to retrieve a game badly begun.'

But Fisher threw himself into the retrieval with demoniac energy, beginning his days at 4 or 5 a.m. Cradock's dangerous situation drew his immediate attention. Although two days earlier the old Admiralty Staff had told Cradock, just before he went into battle, that he could not have any reinforcements, Fisher immediately reversed this decision. '*Defence* has been ordered to join your flag with all dispatch . . .' began Fisher's cable to Cradock in South America. But as Churchill commented, 'we were already talking to a void . . .'.

The first news of Cradock's defeat was received in London with stunned disbelief, and the Admiralty, too, refused to believe the account of the battle from German sources in Valparaiso. Confirmation soon arrived from Captain John Luce of the *Glasgow*. The newspapers were properly solemn, properly laudatory of Cradock's bravery against hopeless odds, and fiercely critical of the Admiralty. It was as well for Battenberg that he had already gone. Embarrassing questions were asked in the House of Lords and the House of Commons. What had happened to the Admiralty? Its criminal ineptitude had endangered Britain's whole maritime strategical arrangements. Already two German cruisers, the *Emden* and the *Karlsruhe*, were disrupting vital British trade in the Indian Ocean and South Atlantic. There now appeared to be no limit to what Admiral von Spee might accomplish by stealth and cunning, and buoyed up by the triumph of his first victory. He might appear any-where—off New York or Newfoundland to destroy Atlantic shipping, off Australia, off the west coast of Africa to support the defence of the German colonies. 'Every vulnerable point all over the world lay exposed to a telling blow from Admiral von Spee,' wrote the official naval historian. And all over the world, Fisher discovered on assuming office, there were scattered individual ships and squadrons any of which might suffer Admiral Cradock's fate. Overnight von Spee had grown from an anxiety and an irritant to the greatest single threat to British sea power. No time could be lost in seeking him out, so that 'whatever might be Admiral von Spee's objective, in whatever quarter he might choose to appear he should find himself confronted with a squadron not merely superior, but so superior as to leave no possible doubt as to the result'.

Soon the Admiralty offices were in a state of tumult, and the vast machinery of direction and administration began to accelerate to the speed of the turbines of Fisher's swift Dreadnoughts. Instructions and memoranda, all in the admiral's sweeping handwriting, spattered with double underlinings and exclamation marks, and headed with his own red-printed RUSH labels, poured from the office of the First Sea Lord. Within six hours of the arrival of news of the Coronel defeat, he had completed arrangements for von Spee's annihilation. Nothing could be accomplished without taking grave risks. It might be considered almost sacrilegious to draw on the Grand Fleet itself for reinforcements; earlier suggestions to this effect had been met with cries of dismay from its Commander-in-Chief Sir John Jellicoe. Fisher did not care a rap for the protests of the Grand Fleet's commanders, and considered their weight of power to be sufficiently superior to that of the German High Seas Fleet. Fisher intended to deprive Admiral Jellicoe temporarily of no less than three of his fastest and most useful ships. Six years earlier Fisher had wrought a revolution in warship design by introducing a giant new form of armoured cruiser, armed with only the heaviest guns and capable of outpacing as well as out-gunning the fastest armoured cruiser in the world. These vessels, these battle cruisers (the *Australia* was one of them) had many detractors, and their vulnerability (for they were only lightly armoured) offered Fisher's enemies a powerful weapon in their continuous assaults on him and his administration. But no one ever built another armoured cruiser: the *Scharnhorst* and the *Gneisenau* were among the last of their kind. Early in the afternoon of November 4th, even before the public knew of the defeat at Coronel, Fisher had sent an order to Admiral Jellicoe to send two of his battle cruisers to the South Atlantic with all speed. They were the *Invincible* and the *Inflexible*, the first-ever battle cruisers, magnificent in profile with their twin tripod masts, their three well-spaced funnels, their eight 12-inch guns and their lean, menacing air about them. Fisher followed this with instructions for another, the *Princess Royal*, to cross the Atlantic and cover the possible emergence of von Spee from the Panama Canal. All these vessels were so much more powerful and so much swifter than von Spee's ships that each could pursue and blow to pieces both armoured cruisers without coming within the effective range of their $8 \cdot 2$-inch guns. One of Fisher's many aphorisms which he loved to quote was 'Tortoises were apportioned to *catch hares. Millions of tortoises can't catch a hare.* The Almighty arranged the greyhound to catch the hare—the greyhound so largely bigger than the hare as to annihilate it! . . .' Fisher's beloved 'greyhounds of the sea' were to have their chance to justify themselves at last.

There were protests, of course. As the admiral who had been threatened with deprival of the *Defence* for Cradock had protested, and got his way, so Jellicoe and his battle cruiser commander, Sir David Beatty, protested at the loss of so much strength. 'Should the High Seas Fleet come out, our need for the missing battle cruisers will be bitterly felt,' complained Beatty. Jellicoe went further and hoped he would 'not be held responsible if the force is unequal to the task devolving upon it'. Fisher brushed aside these pleas, marking Beatty's letter 'Rot! It's gunnery, *not* numbers!' The battle cruisers were to leave the moment they were coaled.

The selection of the officer to lead these battle cruisers into action required deeper consideration. The responsibilities of the command were immense. It covered, in effect, the whole of the Atlantic and Pacific Oceans, and besides the battle cruisers, the commander-in-chief could add to his force the numerous armoured and light cruisers already present in the North and South Atlantic. But the task was not only to seek out and destroy von Spee. The Grand Fleet could not for long be deprived of its great ships. They must be returned, intact, to Jellicoe and Beatty as soon as possible. They would therefore have to avoid any battle damage which might delay their return.

The choice of the admiral by Churchill was a typical masterstroke. Having made clear that he would stay on at the Admiralty as First Lord only if Fisher came as First Sea Lord, he had been acutely embarrassed to hear from Fisher that he would not work with the present Chief of Staff. The public sacking of Sturdee after the news of the Coronel disaster and Prince Louis's resignation would not only disgrace Sturdee, but must also reflect seriously against Churchill's own management of Admiralty affairs. At this point, Churchill was seized with the inspired idea which would save everyone's honour, and his own reputation. He would *promote* Sturdee instead. He would send him off with the battle cruisers to destroy von Spee. Some people were saying that Sturdee as Chief of Staff was most responsible for the death of 'Kit' Cradock; so let him go and avenge it. There would be a nice irony in that, and Sturdee could hardly refuse. The remaining problem was to persuade Fisher that this was the only thing to do. It was not as difficult a task as might be thought. Fisher recognized that the new Board of Admiralty was in a difficult dilemma, with public clamour demanding action and a Chief of Staff who would not go of his own accord. Fisher was a realist, too, with years of experience of political manipulation behind him. Sturdee might be one of his old enemies, as well as a 'pedantic ass' behind a desk. But his sea experience was considerable and he was regarded as a good tactician. The situation and Churchill's proposed solution of it also appealed to Fisher's quixotic sense of humour. Only heaven help the man if he did not polish off von Spee and all his ships smartly, and without any damage to his precious battle cruisers. Sturdee accepted the post with alacrity.

Frederick Charles Doveton Sturdee was fifty-five years old, two years senior to von Spee. In appearance he was short in stature, with a jutting jaw, a massive Roman nose and heavy brows above deep and close-set eyes. He was altogether a less magnificent figure and a less volatile personality than Cradock, and he had never indulged in any of the precipitate adventures which had marked the career of von Spee's previous foe. Caution and perseverence had brought him regular promotion to the rank of rear-admiral in 1910. The lightning decisions and deep intellectual judgment demanded of the post of Chief of Staff were not among his qualities; but he was the very man to wield accurately 'a sledgehammer to crack a nut', as one of his late colleagues at the Admiralty had described the new dispositions against von Spee. Among the men on the lower deck of the navy, who had long been familiar with 'Kit' Cradock's reputation for bravura, he was a nonentity. No one had ever called Sturdee 'Dove'.

The *Invincible* and *Inflexible* were rushed secretly to Devonport, the naval base at Plymouth in south-west England, the moment they had completed coaling, and Sturdee hoisted his flag in the *Invincible* on November 9th. The desperate need for speed appears to have escaped him from the beginning of his new command. The Admiral Superintendent at Devonport considered that he needed until November 13th to remedy some small defects in the ships, and to coal and provision them for their long voyage. Sturdee did not protest. But Fisher was horrified when he heard this news. 'Friday the 13th—what a day to choose!' he exclaimed in the presence of Churchill, who at once sent a signal from London ordering the ships to be completed and away by November 11th at the latest.

Fisher had visualized his battle cruisers pounding their way swiftly down the Atlantic to surprise and exterminate von Spee, perhaps somewhere off the Magellan Straits. The *Invincible* had done over 26 knots on her trials, had more than once managed 28 knots, and more important still, she could steam at 25 knots for days on end, thanks to her new turbine engines and increased boiler power. Admiral Sturdee did not hold with this sort of hustling. Speed was all very well, under exceptional circumstances, but meanwhile he did not wish to overtax his stokers or his engines; nor did he wish to consume coal unnecessarily. So he proceeded south at his ships' most economical speed of ten knots, pausing from time to time *en route* to halt neutral merchantmen to make sure they were not carrying contraband. He coaled again at the Portuguese island of St Vincente in the Cape Verde islands for twenty-four hours, pausing again for some battle practice, and lost another twelve hours when a target towing wire wrapped itself round the flagship's propellers. Later, he diverted from his course to look for the *Karlsruhe*, which was already at the bottom of the sea.

Sturdee appeared to be as unaware of the need for security as for speed. Even before he left, half Devonport knew that the battle cruisers were destined for the south seas: why else the issue of tropical kit to their crews? And Devonport was swarming with German spies. St Vincente, too, was full of Germans, and German ships equipped with wireless. The *Invincible* and *Inflexible* chattered to one another and to other ships on the way. A shore station told the *Invincible* that one of her company had just become a father. Long before they had completed their passage, German spies in South America knew of the imminent arrival of the battle cruisers, and it was common talk in Rio de Janeiro that the English, bent on vengeance, were rushing out the 12-inch-gunned battle cruisers *Invincible* and *Inflexible*.

Only the reports of the gunpower, identity and destination of the ships were correct. Sturdee was still firmly resolved not to hurry the business. He did not arrive at the pre-arranged rendezvous with his other cruisers at Abrolhos Rocks off the coast of Brazil until November 26th. He then set about shipping stores, coaling and conferring with his captains. The search for von Spee was likely to be a long and difficult task, and he knew that the plans for a successful outcome to the venture demanded the most careful planning. Among those present at the meeting, in torrid heat, in Sturdee's day cabin in the *Invincible* was John Luce, the only cruiser commander who had fought von Spee and escaped. The *Glasgow* had been repaired and refitted since Coronel, and Luce and the whole ship's company were thirsting for revenge. John Luce was alarmed both at the leisurely manner in which Sturdee had crossed the Atlantic and the apparent absence of any sort of security. When he heard that Sturdee intended to spend three days at this anchorage before sailing south for the Falkland Islands, he was determined to risk censure by suggesting greater haste and absolute radio silence on the last leg of their voyage. Luce was confident in his own mind that von Spee's destination was also the Falkland Islands, that he was already approaching them, and that he knew of the imminent arrival of the battle cruisers.

'In some trepidation', Luce returned to the flagship after the conference had broken up. There he was received by Sturdee.

'I hope you don't mind me coming over, sir, and please don't imagine I am questioning your orders, but thinking it over I do feel we should sail as soon as possible,' Luce said.

'But dammit, Luce,' Sturdee replied, 'we're sailing the day after tomorrow, isn't that good enough for you? . . .'

There are infinite numbers of fine chances of timing which govern the success or failure of searching warships on the vast expanses of the ocean. No mathematician could have worked out the sum which the computer of fate settled during those next few moments. The anxious and repeated pleas of an impatient captain, and the reluctant agreement of his admiral were to result in the most overwhelmingly decisive sea battle of the First World War. 'Very well, Luce, we'll sail tomorrow. . . .' With those words the sum was complete, the total added up, and the line drawn beneath the figures.

CHAPTER 9

Cape Horn

Two days after Sturdee with his two battle cruisers and his augmented force of armoured and light cruisers left behind him the Brazilian islands of Abrolhos Rocks, von Spee conducted the finishing touches to the Iron Cross presentations off the other side of South America. The eager hurrahs following 'Three cheers for the Emperor' rang out among the giant glaciers of the Gulf of Penas, then anchors were weighed and the squadron with its colliers steamed majestically out into the Pacific. Their bunkers were full and all the ships carried an additional deck cargo of coal for the long voyage round Cape Horn, where there were unlikely to be opportunities for coaling. As a foretaste of what lay ahead for them, they were immediately 'caught up in the swell of a heavy sea coming from the south-west while we received in our faces a proper Cape Horn wind. Ropes were run all over the ship to enable the men to keep their balance. The boats and other heavy objects were double lashed . . . Doors and portholes were secured and the atmosphere on board became cold and humid.'

The weather rapidly worsened as they struggled farther south. All semblance of formation was lost and the squadron and its train broke up into scattered units, none making more than four or five knots. It was bad enough for the *Scharnhorst* and *Gneisenau*. In the *Gneisenau* 'we had to run ropes across the mess deck', wrote one officer. 'Each man took a plate, stumbled across to the counter, received a portion of food, and then squatted in some corner, trying with his plate and mug to adapt himself to the movements of the ship. . . .' The condition of the light cruisers became critical. In the *Leipzig* 'the heavy seas had shifted the deck cargo and all the shoots and scuppers got stopped up with coal so that the water could no longer escape. At times there were three feet of water on deck and we were in imminent danger of capsizing. We turned up into the wind, so as to have our bows to the sea, and the danger was for a time averted. All hands had to turn to and shovel coal overboard . . . standing all the time waist deep in water.'

The loss of coal, so painstakingly loaded only a few days earlier, was serious enough to determine the future movements and timing of the squadron. The effects of the storm went deeper than this. The continuous battering and rolling, the demands of watchkeeping, the difficulty in getting any sleep, led to introspection and gloom among many of the sailors. During those last days in November, the fatalism which their admiral had felt and publicly expressed on the quayside at Valparaiso, for a time spread down to the lower deck. Commander Pochhammer wrote of the mood of the *Gneisenau*'s men at this time: 'Who among us ever thought we should one day be cast upon these southern confines of the earth? The scenes that lay behind us kept passing through our minds! China, Eastern Asia, Tsingtau, what an age since we were there! Ponapé, the declaration of war, how remote it all seemed! The monotonous cruise, under the burning sun, across the infinite desert of waters, how long had it lasted? . . . How long would it thus continue, without rest, without check? . . . How would the end come? In Germany? Or . . . under such a wave as we had just surmounted? Would the spot where we closed our eyes be nameless and our fate remain unknown? . . . Thoughts about life and thoughts about death! I remember that we often spoke of these things at that time, quite openly and naturally. . . .'

The storm eased, and the squadron, still intact and in good order again, rounded Cape Horn on December 2nd. 'Rain clouds hung over jagged islands rising sheer out of the water, at first obscuring our glimpse of the abrupt rock which mounts guard between the Pacific and Atlantic Oceans. . . .' At that moment 'a huge iceberg, coloured pale blue by the sun's rays, appeared on the starboard bow', welcoming them into their new ocean. It was a good omen, and it was a sight that was to be shared by most of the ships' companies. Orders were issued for any who could be spared below to come up on deck to witness the phenomenon. By the evening spirits were higher, and in the *Gneisenau* the cooks brewed a stiff punch for the ship's company from captured French wine.

A second good augury appeared on the horizon soon after the iceberg had disappeared astern, a great four-masted barque, with all sails spread and tacking into the west wind. Von Spee ordered the *Leipzig* to investigate. She was a British ship, the *Drummuir*, loaded with nearly three thousand tons of good coal, many times the amount of coal they had lost in the gale. This was too good an opportunity to miss. The *Leipzig* took the graceful vessel in tow, and the whole squadron sought shelter to devour their prey.

The nearest quiet waters were up the Beagle Channel, named after the famous vessel of Charles Darwin who described this channel as 'a most remarkable feature of the geography of this or any other country . . . about 120 miles long, with an average breadth . . . of about two miles; and is throughout the greater part so perfectly straight, that the view, bounded on each side by a line of mountains, gradually becomes indistinct in the long distance'. It was a happy choice for von Spee. Not only were the savages gone who had made life such a misery for Darwin, but the rocks and land on both sides were swarming with a rich variety of wildlife. Even as they approached Picton Island a pack of large seals glanced anxiously towards the formidable armada advancing towards them and dived into the sea.

While the *Drummuir* was relieved of most of her cargo, her master, J. C. Eagles, came aboard the flagship to meet von Spee. He was by chance an American, a neutral. He was received with apologies by the admiral, who was offered a model of the barque. Von Spee, however, 'courteously declined it and begged him to keep it as a souvenir'.

Picton Island was likely to offer the squadron their last opportunity for relaxation for a long time. Ahead of them now lay only the infinite hazards of the Atlantic, and the inevitability of another battle if they were to attempt the break-through to Germany. Von Spee could not resist the opportunity for his men to rest. It was the least they deserved after winning a decisive battle and suffering one of the worst storms he had ever experienced. The temptations of the wildlife ashore for himself were irresistible, too. He decided there should be a brief holiday.

In the mornings he ordered his pinnace to be hoisted out and he cruised over to the *Gneisenau* to pick up Captain Maerker, his fellow natural history enthusiast, and then proceeded ashore. These were rewarding expeditions. The bird life was marvellously rich and the seals and sea lions were 'of extraordinary size'. Other parties of officers who went ashore, with rifles instead of notebooks, were more intent on a good bag, and shots rang out all along the shore, sending frightened birds of all kinds flying high into the air. It seems that one of these 'a very large and beautiful bird', fell shot into the sea. Von Spee, who did not hold with shooting for sport, had it retrieved. On hearing of this event, a Herr Bloch, a taxidermist and steward in one of the supply ships, asked if he might stuff the bird for his admiral; and this was done.

In the evenings, von Spee enjoyed a game of bridge. Again he would come across to the *Gneisenau*, where Captain Maerker helped to make up a four. On these visits, von Spee wisely abstained from showing any special favours to Heinrich. The young Count would be there to meet him as he came aboard. 'The admiral used to clap him on the back and say a few brief and friendly words.'

Christmas was now less than three weeks away. In addition to their *ersatz* trees, they were now able to decorate the flats and their messes with more foliage gathered ashore. Wild myrtle with its red berries was the favourite. It added a festive air to the austere decks of the warships. Others brought ashore 'souvenirs of Cape Horn' such as colourful stones for paperweights as presents for those at home.

The holiday spirit prevailed until December 6th. Then it was back to business. On that day, the last of the coal was taken from the *Drummuir*, and von Spee convened a conference with his staff and commanders on board the flagship. A sound strategical sense suggested that they should sail east and then north, avoiding the British base at the Falkland Islands, briefly ravaging British trade off the River Plate where it was richest and most vulnerable (the effects of such a successful sortie would be felt for weeks), and then head across the Atlantic for the Cape Verde islands or even the Canaries before running the gauntlet for home. Coal supplies for this operation should prove adequate. When they had left the Gulf of Penas there had been 17,000 tons of coal in their accompanying colliers. More had been ordered through their agents from New York and the Argentine: 25,000 tons in all to be awaiting them at Pernambuco, and another 15,000 tons to be ready to be sent out from New York after January 20. They could hardly hope to reach the neutral waters of the Cape Verde Islands without being reported, and from here all the way home they were certain to be watched. But for the last dash for home they would surely be supported directly, or by diversionary raids, by the High Seas Fleet. It was inconceivable that the German Admiralty would allow them, after all that they had achieved for the Fatherland, to be destroyed so near to home without putting up the sternest resistance.

Almost everyone present at this meeting, including Captain Maerker, agreed that this should be their course of action. The only exceptions were von Schönberg of the *Nürnberg*, von Spee's Chief of Staff, and von Spee himself. These officers were eager to see more action. Von Spee put the case for a positive and aggressive policy, one which would cause direct and long-term political and military damage to British trade and prestige. Since he had taken over command of the East Asiatic Squadron, he had grown ever-stronger in his belief that warfare against the enemy's trade was best conducted by gaining military ascendancy in an area and profiting from this to the utmost, rather than by sinking individual ships. It was for this reason that he had been reluctant to let the *Emden* go. Certainly that gallant ship, from all accounts, had done immense damage in the Indian Ocean. But once she had been caught, the soldiers from India and Australasia, and the vital goods, had sailed freely again. The *Leipzig* and the *Dresden* had done good work, too. But how could the successes achieved by these cruisers working independently be compared with the military triumph of Coronel? At Coronel he had almost wiped out a British squadron; and besides gaining control of half the world's largest ocean, he had struck a fearful moral blow at Britain, shut off all British trade with the east coast of South America, and even closed down Chile's saltpetre mines which had been doing such good business with British shell factories. But paramount to these carefully considered calculations, von Spee was (like his late adversary) a man of action, eager for a *coup*. The target for this *coup* was less than two days' sailing away, at the Falkland Islands. If they were to lose their ships and sell their lives (and von Spee had for long held no illusions on this score), the highest price they could hope for was the capture of a British base. He had witnessed what the British and their allies had done to the German colonies in the Pacific. He had seen the British flag flying from a German flagpost, had heard of the humiliating treatment suffered by a German Governor. The temptation to attack a British colony, raise the German flag over it, and hold as a hostage the British Governor, was irresistible. Moreover, the loss to the British navy of their only coal and supply base in the South Atlantic would be a crippling blow to any squadrons searching for them.

Von Spee placed his more daring plans before his assembled officers. He proposed that they should steam straight for Port Stanley, which he knew to be undefended by shore artillery. The *Nürnberg* and *Gneisenau* were to reconnoitre the harbour in force early on December 8 and report their findings to the main force which would remain out of sight as distant support. The wireless station and mast would then be destroyed by gunfire, and armed parties were to be landed to capture the base and its supplies. There was no reason to suppose that there would be any serious opposition. A recent message passed through the German consul in Punta Arenas asserted that there were no warships in the harbour. This same consul was to be instructed to pass on messages to German citizens in Chile and Brazil who would be prepared to volunteer for garrison duties on the islands. A message was also to be delivered to a Count von Maltzahn, a German baron believed to be resident in Tierra del Fuego, inviting him to accept the appointment of German Governor of the ex-British colony. At the Falkland Islands there were, too, other strictly non-military temptations: the vast numbers of penguins, of which he had read, and the wide variety of bird life, including the sheldgoose.

The same officers argued respectfully against this daring plan, suggesting that speed was imperative and that they should hasten directly to the River Plate estuary where they could rapidly halt British trade, and then steam north-east for home waters. To support their case were the undeniable facts that they had consumed at Coronel 666 rounds of their 8·2-inch shell and had left only 878 rounds. They all agreed that they would not get home without meeting the enemy somewhere. Should they risk their irreplaceable ammunition on the bombardment and possible later defence of a base of no military value to Germany, when they were likely to need all their ammunition in the inevitable battle that lay ahead? Von Spee overruled these reasoned arguments, and before dismissing his commanders ordered the departure from Beagle Channel for noon that day, December 6th.

The squadron left Beagle Channel in bright sunshine and in high spirits. The open Atlantic stretched ahead. After their recent experiences in the Pacific, they felt that this was a more hospitable ocean, providing them with a foretaste of the welcome and celebrations that lay ahead for them at home. However distant this might be, these same waters washed the shores of Europe. But outside the three-mile limit, there came a series of explosions from the pretty *Drummuir*. Her value to them exhausted, she had been towed out and charges had been placed against her hull. The barque went down at once. The sounds were a salutary symbolic reminder that the enemy would be seeking them wherever they sailed.

No hint of the power of the forces being ranged against him had reached von Spee. The fact that he had rounded the Horn, and was already steaming for the same destination as Admiral Sturdee, without receiving any warning message, was a failure of German intelligence as great as its earlier success which had led to victory at Coronel. German agents in Rio de Janeiro knew of the imminent arrival in the South Atlantic of the battle cruisers while von Spee was still in the Pacific. The news had for days been freely discussed in the English Club in Montevideo, and the German intelligence centre in La Plata nearby soon heard it. German agents in Valparaiso also knew what was afoot. The news cannot have failed to reach Punta Arenas. Von Spee had deliberately avoided this remote port in the Magellan Straits for security reasons, but he was within wireless range, passing so close to the western entrance to the Straits that his ships were identified from on shore. The only message von Spee received indirectly from Punta Arenas was the one informing him that Port Stanley was empty of enemy warships. That was all. It is difficult to account for this catastrophic breakdown in the intricate wireless and cable link the Germans had set up in South America. Partly it was the storm. For two days wireless reception was severely limited, and at this time the ships were preoccupied with their own survival. Partly the failure was von Spee's. He had with him three light cruisers whose first function was scouting. It was a tactical error not to send one of them to Punta Arenas, where it could have spread false news of von Spee's whereabouts as well as picking up the latest cables. Nor was it necessary for all three light cruisers to recuperate in Beagle Channel. One of them sent ahead into the Atlantic might well have picked up news by wireless, even from as far away as La Plata, that would offer von Spee some hint of the forces being ranged against him.

The night of December 7th–8th was a beautiful one. Here on the fringes of the Antarctic, it was approaching mid-summer, 'and the visibility of the air, which was to characterize the coming day, seemed at an early hour to be extraordinarily great. At about two o'clock in the morning we were able to distinguish dark masses on the northern horizon. At first we did not know whether it was land or a cloud bank. Soon we were able to recognize their real character: it was land, the Falklands.'

CHAPTER 10

Reconnaissance in Force

The battleship which Cradock had left behind him had finally broken down after all. The engines whose condition had been falsely reported on by a deranged engineer had performed magnificently during the flight south after Captain Heathcoat Grant, her captain, had heard from the *Glasgow* of the destruction of the cruisers. The tubby old *Canopus* had clocked sixteen and a half knots, faster than Cradock had been able to steam in his battle line, and got clean away. Then her boilers had broken down before she could join up with the other cruiser squadron on the east coast of South America. Fisher decided that since she could no longer sail effectively, she would be better employed as a fort. It was a master stroke. Without a base from which to operate and draw supplies, the massive force he was about to concentrate in the South Atlantic would suffer a crippling handicap; and with the defeat of Cradock, the Falkland Islands was wide open to attack by von Spee. It had suddenly become urgently necessary to fortify it. What better defence could there be than the twelve-inch guns of the *Canopus*?

The old battleship limping into Port Stanley was a welcome sight to the frightened people of the colony, whose only defences were three aged pieces of light artillery and some rifles. In rain and bitterly cold gales, Captain Grant set about converting his battleship. First he brought her into the inner harbour, where she was out of sight from the open sea, grounded her, struck topmasts and camouflaged her. Then he had his men drag ashore the battleship's light 12-pounder guns, which were set up in batteries to resist at close range an armed assault. Concealed observation posts were built on the high ground behind the harbour, and these were linked by landline to the 12-inch guns so that they could be fired 'blind'. Old oil barrels were filled with high explosives and strung across the harbour entrance where they could be electrically fired beneath an enemy ship which might survive the fire of the big guns. His own sailors and marines armed and rigidly drilled the islands' farmers, who had been called in to the defence of Port Stanley while their wives and children had been sent far into the interior. A cave in a nearby hill opposite Port Stanley was taken over, provisioned and defended as a last bastion for Sir William Allardyce, his ADC, the colony's few officials, and any who might escape a German invasion.

Even before von Spee had left the Chilean coast for the last time, the *Canopus* which had escaped him on the night of November 1st was well settled into the mud of Port Stanley, ready to do her best with her Victorian guns. The Falkland Island farmers, too, awaited the expected German arrival in better heart. They might not survive but 'we were determined to give von Spee a taste of his own medicine'.

During the last days of November and the first days of December the sense of crisis at Port Stanley deepened. On November 25th the radio station picked up a report that von Spee with his entire squadron had already rounded the Horn. The German admiral was sure to know that Port Stanley was an undefended base, ripe for the picking. It appeared inevitable that he would make an attack before passing on into the South Atlantic. The watch to the south-west was redoubled, but observation was made difficult by the continuing bad weather. Winds of hurricane force driving sleet and hail showers across the islands alternated with periods of calm when low cloud and mist reduced visibility almost to nothing. Conditions could not be better for a surprise attack from the sea.

On the morning of December 7th it seemed that the blow was at last about to fall. Reports arrived at Port Stanley that smoke had been sighted, and that men-of-war were closing the islands from the north. The islanders' anxiety was suddenly and dramatically dispelled. This was not von Spee at all. This was the relieving British squadron, consisting of no less than seven cruisers, two of them great 17,000-ton battle cruisers.

This was a happy day for all the sturdy islanders and their families whose experiences of the war so far had been touched only by disaster. It seemed such a short time since that grey blustery morning when the valiant 'Kit' Cradock had sailed out past Pembroke lighthouse to his doom in his old armoured cruiser. And now, cruising in turn past the same lighthouse came the mighty *Invincible* and *Inflexible,* and the armoured cruisers *Carnarvon, Cornwall* and *Kent,* the modern light cruiser *Bristol,* and the familiar shape of the *Glasgow,* repaired and painted and spruce since her escape from von

Spee. This time the Royal Navy really meant business. Tonight they could sleep soundly in their beds.

As soon as the squadron had anchored in the outer harbour of Port William and Port Stanley, the captains came aboard the flagship for a conference. This took place just twenty-four hours after the meeting of the German captains had broken up with the decision by von Spee to attack the Falklands. The first item on the agenda of Admiral Sturdee's conference was how best to search for the enemy. Sturdee himself was still certain that theirs was to be a long and exhausting hunt. His adversary had, after all, evaded the efforts of the British and her allies' navies to find him in the Pacific. Now the hunting area of his elusive foe was twice as great, and Sturdee had little enough evidence to guide his own future movements. The report which the Falkland Islands had overheard that von Spee had turned the Horn on November 25th could now be recognized almost certainly as a false one, or else he would by now have attacked Port Stanley; although there had been rumours rife in Brazil that he was making for Africa to assist the struggle of the German colonies there. Sturdee was more inclined to accept the unconfirmed intelligence from Valparaiso which indicated that von Spee was still off the Chilean coast, perhaps making for the Panama Canal. He therefore informed his staff and his captains that they would leave in a couple of days time and search up the west coast of South America.

Orders were sent out from the flagship to coal and make any necessary repairs after their long journey. Time was not to be deliberately wasted, but the coaling arrangements suggested no sense of urgency, and were as unhurried as they had been at St Vincente and Abrolhos Rocks, and Sturdee made a signal that the usual wartime precautions could be relaxed and officers allowed ashore. Besides, his own colliers, sent on from Abrolhos Rocks, had not yet turned up as he had hoped and there were only the three already in the harbour from which they could coal. The coal in one of these had deteriorated so badly that it was considered unusable. Also the *Bristol*'s engine troubles were so serious that she had to seek permission to draw her fires. It would therefore take three or four hours for this fast scouting cruiser to be ready for sea. By the late evening of December 7th, therefore, twelve hours after Sturdee's squadron had anchored at the Falklands, only two of his ships were coaling, and only the appointed guardship could be away in half an hour. The rest of the squadron required at least two hours' notice to get under way if an enemy should appear.

At five o'clock on the morning of December 8th, the *Gneisenau* and *Nürnberg* detached themselves from the squadron and their three accompanying colliers and made off at high speed towards the distant smudges of land to the north. It was a perfect dawn, the first clear day for weeks in this storm-racked area between the Antarctic and the South Atlantic, and visibility was unlimited. The landing party in clean white gaiters and armed with rifles had assembled on the *Gneisenau*'s upper deck, and all the men not on duty below were up and peering eagerly towards their destination. Slowly the indeterminate shape of the islands assumed a clear-cut silhouette, and through a telescope it became possible to make out individual bays and headlands and hills. Up on the *Gneisenau*'s bridge Captain Maerker and his navigating officer were taking bearings and marking the chart. There had been a navigation error and it was clear that they would not arrive at the pre-arranged point five miles off Cape Pembroke until 9.30 a.m. Maerker sent a signal to this effect to his admiral and proceeded at higher speed.

Soon after eight o'clock it was possible to make out the wireless masts on the hill near Hooker Point, still far beyond the range of their guns but offering a confirming landmark. The harbour itself, which was cut off from them by Sapper Hill and the long promontory of land reaching out to Cape Pembroke, remained out of sight. Commander Pochhammer was beside his captain on the *Gneisenau*'s bridge. 'The sea was calm, the sky was of azure blue, only a slight breeze from the north-west rippled the surface,' he wrote. 'Then right ahead of us, where the Pembroke lighthouse, built on a low, thrusting tongue of land, marked the entrance, a slender column of smoke appeared, emerging from the sea with all the effect of a mirage; it moved from east to west, towards Port Stanley.' It was the first sign of life from the islands. In the control top high on the *Gneisenau*'s foremast, the ship's senior gunnery officer, Lieutenant-Commander Johann Busche, was ready to direct the ship's guns on to the wireless station. Already his heavy guns had swung in anticipation towards their target. The reports Busche began to telephone down to Captain Maerker on the bridge increasingly suggested that there were other ships in the harbour. Dense clouds of black smoke rose high into the air above Sapper Hill. Were the English burning their coal stocks, as the French had done at Tahiti?

Or was this the smoke from ships rapidly firing up? For the present, it was impossible to tell. At a distance of about ten miles, Busche could definitely make out the slender form of masts above the land. Two of them were moving, this time from west to east, suggesting that one ship was heading slowly for the open sea. The black smoke rose higher and higher, drifting away over the lighthouse. But intermittently through it Busche could make out more masts: four more, then six, then eight. And there were more than that, all of them the masts of warships. The alarming news travelled fast, from Busche himself, down to the bridge below, from there to the wireless room, where it was tapped out to the *Scharnhorst*, hull down over the horizon, and at last to von Spee himself, anxiously pacing the bridge of his flagship.

The identification of the enemy ships was difficult to judge, even at eight miles, but Busche thought that three of them were armoured cruisers of the same class as the *Monmouth*. And there was a light cruiser, too. But there were more masts. These had been obscured before. Now they were suddenly and momentarily clear through his glass. They were thick tripod masts, four of them in all. Three-legged tripod masts. These could mean only Dreadnoughts. Only Dreadnought ships had two tripod masts. Busche's mind turned at once to enemy battle cruisers, their most dreaded foes, and the class of swift heavy-gunned men-of-war the British were most likely to send against them to wreak vengeance for Coronel. When Busche passed his conclusion to Captain Maerker, he was told he must be mistaken: there were no battle cruisers within thousands of miles of the Falklands. But it was possible that there was a battleship in the harbour. Perhaps the one Cradock had so unwisely left behind him. And if there was one, there might be two. This was the intelligence Maerker ordered to be transmitted to von Spee: Stanley Harbour was not empty. The enemy had got there first; and he had a number of cruisers and perhaps two battleships.

The confirmation that there were heavy calibre guns inside Stanley Harbour arrived within a few minutes. A deep boom sounded across the water and two great spouts of water from exploding shells rose into the air on their port beam. The *Gneisenau* had increased speed again to cut off the warship emerging now from behind Cape Pembroke, but when the first salvo of 12-inch shell fell a thousand yards short of him, Captain Maerker ordered a sharp turn away to starboard to evade the next salvo, and battle flags to be hoisted. Almost immediately two more shells landed, this time without exploding. But they were uncomfortably close, and one of them ricochetted from the water and struck the base of the armoured cruiser's fourth funnel.

Von Spee rapidly reconsidered his squadron's situation. Three armoured cruisers and one light cruiser. Against them he had no doubt of the outcome. He could out-gun three ships like the *Monmouth*, blow them to pieces before their own old 6-inch guns were within range. But what of the larger vessels? What class of battleship? He had as much confidence in his engineer staff and his stokers as he had in his guncrews. Against 12-inch-gunned battleships he could never survive. But he could certainly outpace them. It would take the enemy time to clear harbour, and he already had a long lead on them. Von Spee decided to recall the *Gneisenau* and *Nürnberg* without delay and make off at maximum speed to the south-east. The day could not for long remain as clear as this, and every sea mile he covered to the south would bring him closer to the comfort of the Antarctic's mists and fogs. 'Rejoin the flag at best speed,' he signalled to Captain Maerker. All plans for bombardment and invasion, for hoisting the German flag over this British colony, were cancelled by these few words tapped out in morse across the calm, sunlit sea. Once again they were a hunted force.

The helms of the *Gneisenau* and *Nürnberg* were put hard over, and building up quickly to their maximum speed, the two cruisers hastened on a south-easterly bearing to intercept the distant shapes of the rest of the squadron on their easterly course. It took little more than an hour for the squadron to become united. By that time the islands had again become a distant blur on the horizon, the wireless masts which should by now have been shattered by their shell fire had long since disappeared from sight. Only the billowing black clouds of smoke remained as visual evidence of the enemy. But now it no longer hung over Stanley Harbour like some static warning signal of doom. It had broken up and was moving and spread out from the harbour mouth towards the sea. Every minute it spread farther, and at the base of each column of billowing smoke it was just possible to discern high up from the control position of the *Gneisenau*, the small black shape of a speeding warship.

CHAPTER 11

The Beautiful Morning

The look-outs who had been doing duty on watches for some three weeks from the observation post set up on the top of Sapper Hill had never seen such a dawn as on the morning of December 8th. By day and by night they had peered through rain and hail clouds, low-lying mist and for hours through dense fog when they could not even distinguish the sea 450 feet below them. It was exceptional to be able to see five miles from Sapper Hill. This morning visibility was unlimited. But for the curvature of the earth it looked as if it might have been possible to catch distant glimpses of the South American coastline. The first smudge of smoke from the *Gneisenau* and *Nürnberg* appeared through the telescope just after 7.30 a.m. Within ten minutes it was possible to make out four masts, and then the comparative size of the two ships. At 7.45 a.m. the look-out on duty (by chance a Scandinavian, and therefore a neutral) raised the telephone and reported to the *Canopus*, 'A four-funnel and a two-funnel man-of-war in sight steering northwards.' He was mistaken in only one detail: the *Nürnberg* had three funnels but the two forward funnels were set so close together they could easily be confused for one at a great distance.

From the *Canopus* lying on the mud in the inner harbour, it was as impractical to signal visually to the flagship *Invincible* in the outer harbour as it was to observe directly the advancing warships. But the little *Glasgow*, as always, was ready in the right place and at the right time. She was already coaled and so anchored that she was in visual touch both with the *Canopus* and the *Invincible*. The *Glasgow*'s officer of the watch at once had a signalling lamp turned on the flagship to flash out the momentous news to Sturdee. John Luce himself raced up from below, pulling his uniform on over his pyjamas. When he arrived on the quarterdeck there had still been no acknowledgment from the flagship. The *Invincible* had a collier alongside and had recently started coaling. Both she and the *Inflexible* were surrounded by a great rising pall of coal dust, soon to be wrongly interpreted by Captain Maerker and Captain von Schönberg as smoke from burning coal stocks. Why hadn't the signal got through to the flagship yet? John Luce wanted to know. When he heard that they had been trying for five minutes (if they were enemy warships travelling at high speed they would be two miles nearer in that time), John Luce snapped out: 'Well, for God's sake do something about it—fire a gun, send a boat, don't stand there liked a stuffed dummy!' It was Luce's briskness as well as his intelligence which had made the *Glasgow* the most efficient cruiser outside the Grand Fleet.

A three-pounder saluting gun was fired, and a 24-inch searchlight trained on to the bridge of the *Invincible*. At last the message percolated through the screen of coal dust. The flag lieutenant raced down to Admiral Sturdee's cabin. This young officer reported that the admiral was shaving when he burst in with the news. Sturdee himself declared that 'I had just finished dressing'. Other stories have told of his being in his pyjamas and in his bath. It is beyond dispute, however, that he reacted in a calm manner; for, as one of his contemporaries described him, 'he was the least rattled officer I ever knew'. Sturdee himself later recorded, 'I gave orders to raise steam to full speed and go down to a good breakfast.' This was the Sir Francis Drake touch.

If Sturdee considered that von Spee 'came at a very convenient hour', he must have been among the few officers in his squadron who failed to recognize the acute danger of their position. Only the armoured cruiser *Kent* and the *Glasgow* were coaled and ready to leave harbour within an hour or so. The rest of the squadron was either coaling or was carrying out repairs. Before retiring for breakfast, Sturdee had ordered his flag captain to make a general signal: 'Raise steam for full speed. Proceed out of harbour.' But it would take at least two hours for the battle cruisers to cast off their colliers, raise steam and clear the harbour. Meanwhile von Spee could bring up the whole weight of his squadron and subject the anchored ships, who could neither see nor fire accurately on him, to a rain of shells which might well destroy in turn the smaller British ships and seriously damage the more heavily armoured battle cruisers. It was an appalling predicament for the British to be in.

The signal announcing the arrival of von Spee when Sturdee's squadron was coaling arrived at the Admiralty in London shortly afterwards and caused consternation. When the message was brought into Winston Churchill's room, he was deeply concerned. 'We had had so many surprises that these last words sent a shiver up my spine,' he wrote. 'Had we been taken by surprise and, in spite of all our superiority, mauled, unready, at anchor?'

This crucial tactical situation was saved by the old *Canopus*, eschewed by Cradock, crippled by engine troubles both real and imaginary, grounded on mud like some worked-out barge, and now seemingly forgotten by Admiral Sturdee. Captain Grant continued to receive reports from Sapper Hill. More smoke and three more warships were discernible before 9 o'clock, and the first two German cruisers were continuing their approach towards the wireless station at Hooker Point, their guns already trained on their target. Captain Grant and his ship's company had laboured long to prepare their battleship for this moment. His reservist gun crews had trained rigorously whenever the weather had permitted, and all the area of sea within the range of their guns had been divided into marked squares on their charts to facilitate the interpretation of the reports from the observation station. They were all eager to demonstrate their prowess, and perhaps forestall the crippling of Admiral Sturdee's newly arrived squadron. No word came to them from the flagship, so at 9 o'clock Captain Grant sent a signal to the *Invincible* asking leave to open fire. This was given, and the old battleship's 12-inch guns swung round in their turrets and raised their muzzles high into the air, feeling blindly for range and bearing.

The *Canopus* had earlier been due at just this hour to demonstrate to Admiral Sturdee her new-found gunnery skill. Captain Grant had ordered a practice shoot for 9 o'clock, and the crews were eagerly looking forward to the event. It was, too, spiced with a natural element of competition between the two guncrews, the fore and the after turrets. In order to demonstrate their zeal, the crew of the after turret had 'crept out privily by night' and loaded up with practice projectiles ready for the morning 'shoot'. When the rehearsal was suddenly turned into a first night, this crew was hoist with its own petard. The two practice projectiles were already loaded and there was no time to unload.

This competitive enthusiasm was to have a profound effect on the events of the long day that lay ahead. It was the fore turret that was ordered to open fire first. High up on the truck of the foremast of the cruiser *Glasgow* an officer watched the twin 12-inch guns reach up to maximum elevation. 'A cloud of yellow smoke belched from the fore turret of the *Canopus*,' he reported. 'A second later came the crash of the discharge, it seemed an age before two plumes of water like giant cypresses rose high into the air. . . .' The *Gneisenau* and *Nürnberg* were still just beyond the range of the old guns, even at maximum elevation, and the live projectile fell short. A few minutes later, it was the turn of the after turret. The enemy had by then approached a few hundred yards closer. The after turret guns blasted out. Being practice projectiles, they did not explode on impact. They hit the water just short of the *Gneisenau*, and it was one of these which richochetted and struck the base of the armoured cruiser's aftermost funnel, doing little material damage but causing the enemy to retire out of range, and later to flee to the south.

The echo of the *Canopus*'s discharges sent swarms of seagulls from the rooftops of Port Stanley, from the nearby rocks, and from their perches on the masts of the cruisers. Below them as they wheeled about the harbour the men redoubled their efforts to clear the coal from the decks of the battle cruisers, to cast off the colliers and prepare for action. Below decks the engine room artificers and the stokers, called by the bugles sounding 'Action', were all hectically engaged on their complicated and specialized rituals in the artificial light and the heavy atmosphere of oil and grease and coal dust. Theirs were complicated tasks which could be hastened but not skimped, and with all their pent-up enthusiasm, at least two hours must pass before the pressure-gauge pointers swung round their dials and the old reciprocating engines of the armoured cruisers and the newer and more efficient 41,000 horse-power turbines of the *Invincible* and *Inflexible* could thrust into mighty momentum.

The vessel which Lieutenant-Commander Busche had seen from the *Gneisenau* retreating into the harbour was the armed merchantman *Macedonia* which was acting as guardship and was quite unsuitable for battle. Her place was taken by the *Kent*, a three-funnelled aged sister ship of the *Monmouth*, whose silhouette outlined against the setting sun at Coronel had been set so firmly in the memory of all those who had seen her destroyed. A few salvoes from the *Gneisenau*'s 8·2-inch guns could soon have sent her to the bottom, too, and she was hastily recalled when Captain Maerker gave evidence of his intention to attack her.

First away on the pursuit was the dashing little *Glasgow*, whose stokers had made prodigious efforts to get up steam. She threaded her way out from the inner harbour, bustled through Port William where the bigger ships were beginning to weigh, out through the gap in Captain Grant's makeshift minefield, past the lighthouse and into the open sea. There was already a crowd of civilians packed at the best vantage points for the show, and all of them knew the *Glasgow* well and had read of her gallant exploits with Cradock five weeks earlier. It was only proper that she should be in the lead, but at the speed she was attaining (twin white waves building up about her bows) she looked as if she would soon be taking on the full might of von Spee alone.

The *Glasgow*'s company was in a pent-up condition of emotion. The sights they had seen aboard the *Monmouth* that night, the sound of those cheers coming across the waters painted red by the fires consuming the vessel, the sense of shame they had all suffered in the days that had followed, had all left fearful memories in their minds. For the present, the *Glasgow*'s task was to scout, not to immolate herself. John Luce was one of the ablest light-cruiser commanders in the Royal Navy. His was the delicate and hazardous duty of remaining in touch with von Spee, reporting the movements of all his vessels, while avoiding enemy shellfire. For the next hour his signals poured into the flagship's radio room, giving course and position of the *Scharnhorst* and her light cruisers, and the *Gneisenau* and *Nürnberg* who were fast making towards their flagship.

Behind the *Glasgow* the *Kent* remained cautiously awaiting the emergence of Sturdee's big guns, and when the *Carnarvon* and *Inflexible* and then the *Invincible* and *Cornwall* steamed out in stately line past Cape Pembroke soon after ten o'clock, the *Kent* joined them. Already here was a veritable armada: two battle cruisers, three armoured cruisers, and a light cruiser. And still there remained the *Bristol*, struggling to get some heat from her drawn fires. If this great force of men-of-war with their overwhelming weight of broadside could once get within range of von Spee's squadron, the only result must be an annihilation more appalling than Cradock's at Coronel.

The East Asiatic Squadron was rapidly building up to its maximum speed and by 10.30 a.m. the two groups of cruisers were only a few miles apart on their closing courses. Few of the German officers at this time seem to have experienced any sense of alarm at their situation. It was most regrettable that the operation against the islands had had to be abandoned, and some of them felt that they should have concentrated their forces and subjected the harbour to a bombardment, even at the risk of later finding themselves short of ammunition when they might be in need of it. But their admiral had decided otherwise, and he had been right on every occasion since they had left Tsingtau more than five months ago. There was little doubt among any of the German officers that they could evade all but the light cruisers which might be sent in pursuit of them. One of them, easily identifiable as the *Glasgow* which had fled from them at Coronel, was already approaching the maximum range of the *Gneisenau's* heavy guns. But there was nothing to fear from her. Behind her, and just emerging from behind Cape Pembroke, a towering black mountain of smoke marked the progress of the main cruiser force, yet obscured the identity of its ships. From the bridge of the *Gneisenau* Captain Maerker, Commander Pochhammer and more of the ship's officers were all straining their eyes in an effort to distinguish the number and spacing of the funnels and their position in relation to the masts, the silhouette of bridge or gun turret, any feature which would help to guide them to the right page of their ship identification reference books.

They were in the act of joining forces with the *Scharnhorst*, *Dresden* and *Leipzig* when the truth at last became evident. 'Two vessels soon detached themselves from the number of our pursuers,' wrote Pochhammer. 'They seemed much bigger and faster than the others, as their smoke was thicker, wider and more massive. All glasses were turned upon their hulls, which were almost completely enveloped by the smoke.' Lieutenant-Commander Busche had been right. Both of these great ships had tripod masts. And their smoke was streaming from three funnels. These were no old battleships like the *Canopus*. These were Dreadnoughts. Nor were they battle-ships at all, which they could have outpaced. Tripod masts and three funnels meant battle cruisers. No British battle cruiser carried fewer than eight 12-inch guns, and every British battle cruiser could steam five knots faster than they could. It was 'a very bitter pill for us to swallow. We choked a little at the neck, the throat contracted and stiffened, for this meant a life and death struggle, or rather a fight ending in honourable death. . . . It would have been senseless to harbour any illusions, for the sky remained clear; there was not the smallest cloud to be seen, nor a wisp of fog to throw over us its friendly mantle.' Now that the truth was known, it was the duty of every officer to conceal from the men any doubts he might feel about the outcome of the battle that lay ahead. This was a time for steel resolution and determination to put aside fears and doubts. For the captains of the five ships, this testing time was even sterner. They had no one in whom they might confide. Nor had Maximilian von Spee himself. This was the hour when Kaiser Wilhelm's orders must be remembered, and repeated again and again: 'The officer in command . . . must constantly bear in mind that the efficiency of the crew and their capacity to endure privations and dangers depend chiefly on his personality. . . . The more difficult and desperate the position, the more strictly the officer must adhere to the laws of military honour. . . .'

The extraordinary weather conditions provided the final note of confirmation that on this morning fate had turned everything against them. On almost any day but this there would have been fog banks or at least a succession of low-lying squall clouds which would have provided them at least with the temporary concealment they needed to make confusing alterations of course and cover their retreat. Now only speed and more speed could save them, and the long chance that a lucky hit by their heavy guns at maximum range might slow up their adversaries.

Then of course the whole conception of this attack had been wrong. If they had arrived in concentration at first light a couple of hundred shells would have created havoc in the harbour. Or if they had sent in one of the light cruisers to reconnoitre, keeping the main force well beyond the horizon, they would have had warning in plenty of time to steam away to safety. It was too late for considerations like these. The day was young and clear. The pack was in full cry.

CHAPTER 12

The Brave Sailors

No one who saw the *Invincible* and *Inflexible* working up to full speed that morning ever forgot the sight. A special kind of *mystique* had grown up around the battle cruiser. To the impressive dimensions and gunpower of the Dreadnought battleship, themselves so stirring in profile, and in the pugnacity of their demeanour, was added the magnificence of unprecedented speed. For some six years now the summation of maritime power had been invested in the battle cruiser, thundering through the seas at twenty-five knots, guns trained towards an unseen enemy. Here was a spectacle of strength and belligerence the like of which the world had never before seen. When the *Invincible* hoisted the 'General Chase' flag, the most stirring of all signals, the picture was complete and perfect. There was the enemy squadron, hull down in flight, five smudges of smoke marking the five ships which had humbled the Royal Navy and killed 'Kit' Cradock and nearly two thousand of their comrades. It was a moment of purest elation for the companies of the two battle cruisers and the armoured cruisers which were struggling to hold the pace. The men of the *Invincible* and *Inflexible* had washed off the stains of coaling in preparation for battle and been ordered down to an early mid-day dinner. But all those who were not slaving down in the boiler rooms and engine rooms had only grabbed chunks of bread and come up on deck to watch the spectacle.

They had been making twenty-six knots, the 'white streaks at stern and the water boiling in their wakes, often higher than the poop deck, masses of black oily smoke from the funnels, against which the many white ensigns showed up in striking contrast'. But then Admiral Sturdee had ordered a reduction in speed, first to twenty-four and then to nineteen knots, for his force was becoming scattered. For eighty minutes Sturdee held back, as if reluctant for battle without support, while his older ships came up with him.

They were no longer gaining on von Spee and there was impatience aboard the battle cruisers. What was their admiral doing?

He could surely not be afraid of going into action alone against these hopelessly outclassed Germans? A sentence from the Fighting Instructions Sturdee had prepared on the voyage out from Britain had clearly stated that 'the main duty of the battle cruisers is to deal with the armoured cruisers'. Why, then, the delay? They were powerful enough to deal with the whole of the enemy force without risk of serious damage. At 12.20 p.m. Sturdee changed his mind, to everyone's relief. The *Carnarvon* was barely making eighteen knots and the *Kent* and *Cornwall* were not doing much better. From a magnificent stern chase the action had turned into a game of follow-my-leader, and the German squadron was still well beyond the range of their largest guns. The day was already more than half spent, and not a single shot had yet been fired. Sturdee at last gave orders for the *Invincible* and *Inflexible*, and the little *Glasgow* still scouting three miles ahead, to work up to twenty-six knots again. But perhaps they were already too late?

Once again the five dark scurrying shapes began to grow larger, even to the naked eye. Through glasses it was possible to observe that von Spee was altering slightly to starboard to widen the distance from his pursuers, who were on a parallel course. At the same time, the compact formation he had so far held showed signs of breaking up. One of the light cruisers appeared unable to hold the pace and was lagging behind. But it was difficult to be sure, for the Germans were steaming direct before the wind and their own smoke was blowing along with them. When the time came to open fire, ranging and spotting was going to be difficult. Von Spee had gained another tactical advantage over his enemy.

By 12.45 von Spee had turned further to the south, and Sturdee in following these changes found himself almost dead astern of the enemy and able to bring only eight of his sixteen heavy guns to bear. His own smoke added to his embarrassment. It was tending to blow along with them, too, and the oil being sprayed on to the fires to increase the power of the turbines made conditions especially difficult for the rangetakers and spotters. In spite of these difficulties and the fact that they were not yet within range of the lagging German cruiser, Sturdee ordered the signal 'Open fire and engage the enemy.'

The decks were now clear of spectators, and every man was at his post. At almost precisely one o'clock and at a range of 16,500 yards, or rather over nine miles, the *Inflexible* fired the first two-gun salvo of the battle. The great 12-inch guns were 'on their stops' (at maximum elevation) in the fore turret of the battle cruiser, the muzzles spat a yellow tongue of flame, and the two shells (each weighing a third of a ton) arched up in their trajectory, soaring thousands of feet into the sky before descending towards their target. They fell far short of the last of the German ships. The *Invincible* joined in, with equally unsuccessful results. Each fall of shot and its towering fountain of water was well short. The flagship's gunnery officer, Lieutenant Edward Dannreuther, watched the splashes through his big binoculars from high up in the fore top, and realized that a few more minutes must pass before he could hope for a hit. He had calibrated his guns at 12,000 yards on the voyage out from England. They had never before considered shooting even at this range; now they were attempting to strike the enemy at a distance some three miles greater. Long distance gunnery was still in its infancy in the Royal Navy.

From the *Glasgow*, ahead and on the port bow of the flagship, the shooting appeared deplorable. 'We were all dismayed at the battle cruisers' gunnery, the large spread, the slow and ragged fire,' wrote Lieutenant Harold Hickling. 'An occasional shot would fall close to the target while others would be far short or over. . . . "At this rate," I said . . . "it looks as if Sturdee and not von Spee is going to be sunk." "It's certainly damn bad shooting," he replied.'

The *Leipzig*, the trailing German cruiser, was straddled as the range continued to close. Then when a shell burst just ahead of her bows and she sailed at full speed through the fall of water, it appeared as if she had been hit. But she emerged again a few seconds later, her gun crews drenched but unscathed. What a contrast this was to the German shooting under the appalling conditions at Coronel! But this time von Spee was intent on holding his fire and preserving his precious ammunition until he could be sure of committing damage. His 8·2-inch turret guns could range almost as far as the British 12-inch. But look how the British were wasting their ammunition! By 1.15 p.m. the British fire was as irregular and still without pattern. Now that the range had closed further, overshooting shells were falling near the other ships, too. Soon the law of averages must result in a hit on one of his light cruisers. A single lucky 12-inch shell was enough to shatter the *Leipzig*. And they had not one more knot of reserve speed on which they could draw.

Von Spee made the decision to split his force at 1.20 p.m. They were still unscathed, they had still not fired a shot. He would take his two armoured cruisers out to meet the enemy and engage in a gun duel, detaching his light cruisers at the same time. '*Dresden, Nürnberg, Leipzig* leave the line and try to escape,' he ordered. Their captains knew exactly what to do. He had the utmost confidence in them, and they might well have the speed to hold off the old British armoured cruisers until nightfall, even if the *Glasgow* could catch them. In quick succession the *Dresden, Nürnberg* and *Leipzig* swung out of line to the south, flashing patriotic good wishes and a last farewell to von Spee. They made no attempt to hold any sort of formation because concerted action was out of the question. Their survival depended on the condition of their bearings, on the degree of wear on a thousand moving parts, the state of their boilers, and quality of the coal in their bunkers, and above all on the physical endurance of their stokers. Even in this era of mechanical warfare, of high-explosive shells which could hit a target at ten miles, the sheer muscle power of a handful of men could still count as decisively as in the days of Actium.

Before his light cruisers disappeared from sight to the south, von Spee could see that it was not Otto's ship the *Nürnberg* which was proving herself the fastest. If any of the light cruisers were going to escape (and the *Glasgow* and three armoured cruisers were hard on their heels) it would be the *Dresden*. She was the newest of the three and had always proved herself the nippiest. Already it looked to von Spee as if the Countess might this day lose both her sons as well as her husband.

The moment von Spee had detached his three little cruisers, the *Scharnhorst* and *Gneisenau* turned like cornered animals steadying themselves for the combat that might save their young. To those aboard the British battle cruisers it appeared certain that the superior weight of their metal would in the end be decisive; and as neither of the German captains would surrender their ships under any circumstances, few of them were likely to survive.

But was this, after all, a turn towards certain destruction? The statistics were overwhelmingly loaded in favour of the British. The total weight of broadside the *Invincible* and *Inflexible* could bring to bear was over 10,000 pounds, the *Gneisenau* and *Scharnhorst* less than 3,500 pounds. And the battle cruisers had already shown their superiority in speed. Yet there were certain factors in favour of von Spee. John Luce himself had witnessed the remarkable accu-

HMS *Inflexible*, as first completed. Sturdee's flagship was similar (*Imperial War Museum*)

16 Five smudges of smoke on the horizon betray the fleeing East Asiatic Squadron, while (bel Admiral Sturdee's flagship *Invincible*, in the foreground, steams in pursuit from Port Stanl In the background is the *Glasgow*, facing her second battle, on the left the armoured cruise *Kent*, in the centre the *Inflexible* (*Imperial War Museum*)

(*Above*) HMS *Invincible* working up to full speed. (*Below*) Fisher's 'greyhounds' pursuing
von Spee south of the Falkland Islands (*Imperial War Museum*)

18 A scattering of survivors from the *Gneisenau* being rescued by boats from the *Inflexible* (*Imperial War Museum*)

racy of the German gunfire even at great range and under adverse
weather conditions at Coronel. He had also seen how rapidly the
German guns could be worked, as fast as four rounds a minute
when the fight was at its hottest, while the British 12-inch guns had
not bettered a round every thirty seconds. If von Spee could close
the range so that his 5·9-inch guns could become effective, then he
might well make the two British ships suffer, for they carried only
4-inch secondary armament—'those wretched peashooters', as
critics had called them. Above all, in any naval action, it was,
according to Lord Fisher's often repeated exclamation, '*Gunnery!*
Gunnery!! Gunnery!!!' that would count. And so far Sturdee's
gunnery had been deplorable.

The gunnery duel began at 1.30 p.m. at a range of about 14,000
yards. Von Spee led the *Gneisenau* first on an easterly course, and
then when Sturdee followed his turn, he altered course inwards
towards the enemy another four points. Now for the first time all
four ships could bring their full broadsides to bear. For a few salvoes
the German shells fell short, then as the range closed the skilled
and experienced rangetakers and gunlayers found their form, and
the gun crews found their rhythm. 'The German firing was magnificent to watch,' reported one British officer, 'perfect ripple salvoes
all along their sides. A brown coloured puff with a centre of flame
marking each gun as it fired. . . . Their shooting was excellent; they
straddled us time after time.' In less than fifteen minutes, the
Scharnhorst scored her first hit on the *Invincible*. Sturdee at once
turned his flagship two points away from the enemy, as if flinching
from the blow and bringing himself beyond the effective range of
the German guns.

The British gunnery remained irregular and the waterspouts
about the German ships continued to be widely dispersed. Their
own smoke was partly to blame for their inaccuracy. Sturdee had
again been forced into a tactically weak position. In spite of his
greatly superior speed, the north-westerly wind, combined with his
own course and position in relation to the enemy, was cloaking the
Inflexible in a black cloud, and even masking his own after turret.
For almost half an hour he was like a half-blinded heavyweight
fighting a bantamweight, suffering blows which he could not return,
although two hits were made on the *Gneisenau* and another on the
Scharnhorst, none of which did fatal damage. By two o'clock a
ridiculous *impasse* had been reached which suggested that the battle

had declined into a stalemate before it had really warmed up. In spite of the continuing limitless visibility, Sturdee could no longer see von Spee, and in his efforts to clear his own smoke and avoid further damage had taken himself beyond the range of his own guns, too. A total silence fell over the sea.

Admiral Sturdee felt impelled to do something to work his way out of this dilemma, so he brought his two battle cruisers sharply round to starboard in an attempt to free himself from his own blinding smoke and get on the lee side of his opponent. It was a manoeuvre that entirely closed off the intermittent glimpses he had been getting of the German cruisers, and he never saw von Spee turn more sharply on to a due southerly course. When Sturdee at last emerged from his own smokescreen, he could observe only the sterns of the *Gneisenau* and *Scharnhorst*, making off at best speed and already far beyond range. He was in precisely the same relative position to his foe as he had been two hours earlier, and he now faced another long stern chase before he could again open fire. The British admiral had been neatly out-manoeuvred and was now in real danger of losing his enemy. Still the sun shone from a cloudless sky, but it was almost unprecedented for these conditions to continue until sunset, and when the bad weather arrived, it would come up from the south. As the *Gneisenau*'s first officer noted, 'Every minute we gained before nightfall might decide our fate. The engines were still intact and were doing their best. . . .'

The long lull allowed all the protagonists to rest and repair their damage. Forty minutes passed. The *Invincible* and *Inflexible*, streaming even denser clouds of black smoke as they strained after their quarries, slowly grew larger again as they approached the Germans from astern on the port side. Through glasses from the bridge of the *Gneisenau* it was possible to see the forward 12-inch guns of both battle cruisers reaching up to their maximum elevation and pointing directly at them. Then the two big enemy ships altered course a couple of points to port to bring more of their guns to bear. At 2.50 p.m. the familiar brown puffs with their scarlet and white hearts sprang out from eight and a half miles away, and seconds later came the chorus of screams from the falling shells and the always startling eruptive growth of water columns about them. A very refined and cool form of courage was called for among the gunlayers, the spotters and rangetakers to busy themselves efficiently with the special instruments of their trade during these thunderous moments, and with the spray of near misses falling about them.

The range was down to 15,000 yards, and von Spee knew that he must again attempt to close it if his own fire was to have any effect on the armoured sides and decks of the British ships. He held on for five minutes. The enemy's shooting was better this time, for their lenses were less obscured by smoke. But still no hits were scored. The *Scharnhorst* and *Gneisenau* edged further to port, and at 2.55 p.m. swung across hard to port in order both to close the enemy and attempt to cross his bows: the classic evolution of 'crossing the enemy's "T"'. At the same time both German ships opened a steady, well-directed fire. Every possible means of escape had been exhausted. With all the cunning in the world, no admiral could get away with repeating an earlier trick. The skills of gunnery and simple courage must now combine with the cold statistical figures of range and weight of shell, muzzle velocity and penetrating power: these were among the final arbiters in a gunnery duel when further tactical evasion was impossible.

The second gun duel was a repeat of the first. The four big ships were again steering on an easterly converging course which soon allowed von Spee to bring his secondary armament into play. Again the German gun crews might have been competing for the Kaiser Cup, salvo following salvo with clockwork precision, the minute adjustments for range following the spotters' reports. It was a magnificent display, and the hits on Sturdee's ships followed in rapid succession, although the ugly flash and puff of smoke from a hit, instead of the tall column of erupting water, showed the English that the *Gneisenau* and *Scharnhorst* were suffering too.

The Battle of the Falkland Islands was at its height at three o'clock. The deep thunder of the guns and the whine of falling shells were continuous, and the sea about the racing hulls of the adversaries was in a white concussive turmoil. At this moment a tall and beautiful sailing ship appeared suddenly from the east, 'with all sail set, including stunsails, passing down between the two squadrons. A truly lovely sight she was,' one British officer recalled, 'with every stitch of canvas drawing as she ran free in the light breeze, for all the world like a herald of peace bidding the two lines of grim warships cease the senseless destruction. . . .' She was a Frenchman, it was later reported, 'ignorant of the outbreak of war as she had left Europe in July'. Her unintended arrival occurred at the culminating point of the battle. She could not have better timed her entrance. And yet there was still something improper about her appearance at all at this hour, like the eager curiosity of a cameraman at any savage death struggle. However magnificent and awe-inspiring the slaughter might be, this was no moment for uninvolved witnesses. When she turned hastily about, the crash of the guns continued as if she had been only the ghost ship of a hundred sea legends.

During all this phase of the action, fought out between 10,000 and 14,000 yards, both sides were hitting each other again and again. The German gunnery remained steadier and more regular, but the lighter shells, descending in a steep trajectory, were breaking up on the battle cruisers' upper works and doing little military damage to the ships. Safe from the light German shell behind their armour plate, not one British gun had been put out of action, and not one British sailor had been wounded. By contrast, the British 12-inch lyddite shell was tearing through the decks of the German ships and doing great execution among the crews. The *Gneisenau*'s 5·9-inch casemate guns were keeping up a regular fire, but the casualties were mounting up there as they were everywhere in the ship. 'Every casemate presented the same picture,' reported the officer in charge of this battery. 'The men with powder-blackened faces and arms, calmly doing their duty in a cloud of smoke that grew denser as the firing continued: the rattling of guns in their mountings; the cries of encouragement from the officers; the monotonous note of the order transmitters, and the tinkle of the salvo bells. Unrecognizable corpses were thrust aside, and when there was a moment, covered with a flag. . . .'

The *Scharnhorst* was taking the worst of the punishment. She was on fire and listing, and had lost her third funnel by 3.10 p.m. But again the fire from the German ships was giving Sturdee anxiety. If only he could see to swat at the wasps that were plaguing him. If only he could get on the lee side of the enemy ships, surely he could at last finish them off. By now his superiority in speed must be at least ten knots. So the admiral decided again to break off the action and clear his smoke. He accomplished this by taking his two ships through a complete circle at 3.15 p.m. When the *Invincible* and *Inflexible* emerged from their own pollution, the German ships were again far to the south and temporarily out of range. And at last the weather was breaking in the favour of the Germans, with grey rain clouds coming up from the south. 3.40 p.m. was for von Spee the decisive moment of the battle. At this time the two

German ships were on a south-westerly course, still struggling to derive from shattered boilers and engine rooms the power to escape, and still struggling to defy the renewal of pulverizing broadsides from the two British battle cruisers, now six miles away on a north-westerly bearing and on a parallel course. A splinter had severed the halyards of von Spee's flag. Captain Maerker noticed this and became anxious about his admiral. The *Gneisenau* managed to signal 'Why is the admiral's flag at half mast? Is he dead?' The upper decks of the *Scharnhorst* were a shambles and it seemed probable that the C-in-C and all his staff had perished.

But the reassuring message came back promptly: 'I am all right so far. What have you hit?'

'The smoke is so bad it is impossible to tell,' Maerker replied.

The British battle cruisers had opened fire again, at closer range and clear of smoke. The effect was stunning. The air seemed to be torn asunder by the succession of explosions, and the two German ships could scarcely see one another through the curtain of waterspouts. But von Spee managed to get a message through to his old friend, who only forty-eight hours earlier had so strenuously opposed the Falkland Islands attack which had brought them to disaster. There was not much to be said now, just a brief and generous apology: 'You were right after all.'

The *Inflexible* had been half blinded and frustrated by Sturdee's smoke since the very beginning of the action. But as a result of clumsy manoeuvring by the flagship during the last complete turn, the second battle cruiser emerged leading the line. This gave the *Inflexible*'s gun crews the opportunity of which they had so far been deprived. 'For the first time I experienced the luxury of complete immunity from every form of interference,' the battle cruiser's gunnery officer said. 'I was now in a position to enjoy the control officer's paradise: a good target, no alteration of course and no next aheads or own smoke to worry me.' The effect of the *Inflexible*'s lyddite shell on the *Scharnhorst* was fearful to behold. 'Her upper works seemed to be but a shambles of torn and twisted steel and iron, and through the holes in her side, even at the great distance we were from her, could be seen dull red glows as the flames gradually gained the mastery between decks.'

The *Invincible* again succeeded in positioning herself relative to her sister ship so that her smoke created the maximum interference, and the *Inflexible*'s guns were soon masked once more. But not for long. Like the *Good Hope* at Coronel the *Scharnhorst* was making a dying lunge at her torturers, straight towards them. On her own initiative the *Inflexible* doubled back and opened a murderous fire on the blazing hulk. Yet the flagship was still firing, and with remarkable regularity; would she never sink? 'One could see the "twinkle" of her gun discharges, as she continued to fire the most perfect salvoes,' the *Inflexible*'s gunnery officer recorded. 'I remember asking my rate operator, "What the devil can we do?"' High above the guns of the *Invincible*, Lieutenant Dannreuther, a member of a notable musical family and a godson of Wagner, was appalled by the sight of the German flagship. 'She was being torn apart and was blazing and it seemed impossible that anyone could still be alive.' Not even the most fearsome passage from one of his godfather's operas could have matched the savagery he was witnessing.

The only relief the *Scharnhorst* was gaining from this continued onslaught was from the near misses, which sent tons of water through the holes in her sides and damped down the fires. The relief from this remedy was brief. The weight of water increased the flagship's list and further slowed her. By 4.10 p.m. she was scarcely moving. 'Notwithstanding the punishment she was receiving,' reported Sturdee, 'her fire was wonderfully steady, and accurate, and the persistency of her salvoes was remarkable.'

How could anyone be left alive to feed the guns under these conditions? And then, when all who were watching her death throes had begun to despair, '*Scharnhorst* suddenly shut up as when a light is blown out'. She turned over on her beam, all flags still flying, and sent a last message to the *Gneisenau* who gave evidence of coming to her aid. Keep away and try to save yourself, it said.

Commander Pochhammer watched his flagship's last moments from the conning tower of the *Gneisenau*. 'She heeled gradually over to port and her bows became more and more submerged,' he wrote. 'Her forward turret was about $6\frac{1}{2}$ feet above the water when it fired its last shot. Then, with her screws still turning, she slid swiftly into the abyss, a few thousand yards astern of us. A thick cloud of smoke from her boilers shot up above her grave as high as her masts. It seemed to be telling us, "*Scharnhorst* awaits *Gneisenau*". A feeling of utter loneliness, as if one had lost one's best friend, came over everyone who had witnessed the end.'

Not a soul survived from the German flagship. The *Gneisenau* was making off as well as she could to the south-west and the rain clouds which were coming up, but much too slowly, to meet her. She was firing as she went, and there could be no thought of searching for survivors while the battle was still on. The *Gneisenau* survived for nearly two hours, displaying incredible ruggedness in her structure as well as courage of the highest order among her crew. Still intermittently handicapped by their own funnel smoke, the *Invincible* and *Inflexible*, sometimes together, sometimes alone, twisted and turned off the armoured cruiser's starboard quarter, shooting at ranges where they were almost immune from the few surviving heavy and medium calibre guns of the cruiser. The pace of the ships had now so reduced that the old *Carnarvon*, who was too slow to pursue the light cruisers, came up with the battle, and added her own broadsides to those of the battle cruisers.

The *Gneisenau* continued to resist almost to the end, although few of her guns could be worked and her ammunition ran so low that she had to resort to practice shell which could not seriously damage the enemy. In spite of the overwhelming volume of fire being directed at her from three ships on three different bearings, she got a last shot into the *Invincible* at 5.15 p.m. It only dented her armour belt.

Fifteen minutes later, Sturdee watched the *Gneisenau* turn towards him, as the *Scharnhorst* had done earlier, 'with a heavy list to starboard . . . with steam pouring from her escape pipes, and smoke from shell and fires rising everywhere. About this time I ordered the signal "Cease fire", but before it was hoisted the *Gneisenau* opened fire, and continued to fire from time to time with a single gun.'

The visibility had suddenly reduced, a drizzling rain was already falling, two hours too late. It was the treacherous weather's final mocking gesture. Captain Maerker and his Number One were both still alive. But three-quarters of the ship's company were dead or wounded, the engines had expired, there was not a shell left. There was to be no surrender; such an act was still unthinkable. Captain Maerker ordered the survivors on deck and gave instructions for his ship to be flooded. 'The cannonade gradually died down,' his Number One recalled. 'It was now up to us not to let the floating ship fall into the enemy's hands and to preserve as many survivors as possible for the Fatherland. . . . The men left their stations in perfect order and the wounded comrades were carried above. Hardly any companion-ways or ladders were left but masses of

crumpled steel offered sufficient support for climbing on to deck. . . .'
The stokers and engine room personnel emerged, 'coal-blackened
from furnaces and bunkers', through any holes they could find in
the decks, and, numbed and quiet after the hell of the last four-and-
a-half hours, made their way to the side and the shattered fragments
of the boats. Before they started to throw over rafts and hammocks
and any length of timber they could find, Captain Maerker appeared
on what remained of the bridge. He shouted orders for three cheers
for 'His Majesty the Emperor' and for 'Our good and brave *Gneisenau*'. The voices of the sailors rose briefly above the multiple chorus
of sound that emerges from any sinking man-of-war—the hissing
of steam, the crackle of fires, the distant and sinister boom of small
internal explosions, the cries of the wounded. 'Deutschland,
Deutschland über alles . . .' followed the cheers before the order
to abandon ship was passed from end to end.

The *Gneisenau* went down a few minutes past six o'clock. As she
revealed her red underside, men could be seen walking down it into
the water, and when she went under she left behind her struggling
in the sea some four hundred of her company, many of them
wounded. For the wounded there was little chance of survival, for
the shock of the immersion in the cold water alone was enough to
kill them. But even for the fit and unwounded, the weather had one
last cruel trick to play. Besides the drizzle, the temperature had
suddenly fallen and a cold wind had got up, bringing with it dangerously choppy waves that tossed them about and threw them from
their perches on spars and makeshift rafts. Within a few hours a freak
warm summer's day had been transformed into a chill Antarctic
dusk.

This time rescue work could safely be carried out. It was a
lengthy and difficult business. Many of the battle cruiser's boats
had been riddled by shellfire, and the *Carnarvon* was unaccountably
slow in lowering hers. The last sombre scenes of the main action
were played out alongside the *Carnarvon* soon after seven o'clock.
The ship's whaler was returning, loaded with survivors, some
wounded and others half dead with cold. The rising seas took hold
of the whaler as it was coming alongside and smashed it against the
steel plates of the cruiser. 'One of our cutters was near,' wrote a
midshipman, 'and managed to rescue all our men, but some of the
Germans floated away calling for help which we could not give them.
It was shocking to see the look on their faces as they drifted away and

we could do nothing to save them. A great many were drowned. . . .
We could see them floating past, a horrible sight.'

Young Heinrich von Spee was not among the survivors of the
Gneisenau. His brother died about an hour and a half later, some
seventy-five miles to the south-east. The *Nürnberg*'s failure to
escape was the worst piece of bad luck in a long day of misfortune
for the East Asiatic Squadron. Her pursuer was the old armoured
cruiser *Kent*. Earlier in the chase, by straining her boilers and the
muscles of her stokers to the utmost, the *Kent* had made enough
headway to open fire. Her 6-inch shells fell short, while the answer-
ing fire from the *Nürnberg*'s little 4·1s insultingly overshot their
target. By 5 p.m. a cold mist and occasional drizzle were obscuring
the *Kent*'s hustling quarry, and the old reciprocating engines of the
British ship were vibrating so badly that the rangefinders were
unusable. Within the next half-hour despair on the *Kent*'s bridge
changed to hope, and then to certainty of action after all. The
Nürnberg unaccountably began to lose speed: two of her boilers had
burst from the strain of nearly eight hours under unprecedented
pressure. A close-fought gun duel followed, with the inevitable end
for the unarmoured little German ship, although she had pumped
some forty shells into the *Kent* before she went down. Two of the
British cruiser's boats were hastily despatched to search for survivors
before darkness closed over the scene. 'A few men were found
floating lashed to hammocks,' Sir Julian Corbett recorded, 'but
many of these were dead from the cold, and albatrosses were
attacking even the living. In the end only seven men were saved
alive.'

The *Leipzig* fought as valiantly to the end as the *Scharnhorst*,
Gneisenau and *Nürnberg*. Although the 6-inch guns of the *Cornwall*
finally did for her, it was the cunning tactics of John Luce in the
Glasgow that allowed both British cruisers to come up with their
adversary. Luce had the speed of her from the beginning, and he
kept firing with his forward gun from astern until the *Leipzig* was
forced to turn in order to bring her broadside to bear. Each time
the old *Cornwall* was able to reduce her distance, and at 4.17 p.m.
opened fire. The *Leipzig* fought the two superior British ships until
her ammunition was exhausted and all her torpedoes fired. Again
there were the same scenes of gallantry and patriotism before she
went down in the darkness at 9.23 p.m.: the anxious enquiries of

the wounded who wished to be reassured that the flag was still flying; the comforting of the dying; the speech by the captain; the cheers and the singing against a backcloth of flames and twisted metal; and then at last the survivors diving into the icy, choppy sea. To the rescuers, it was remarkable that as many as eighteen were brought back alive.

Only the flying *Dresden* and one of the supply ships (the American master of the *Drummuir* was luckily aboard her) escaped from that awful day of destruction and death. Only the *Dresden* was fast enough to reach the shelter of the mists and low rain clouds that had hung back so cruelly all day. By the middle of the afternoon, her pursuers knew that she could never be caught, and diverted their attention to her slower consorts. It took nearly three months to hunt the *Dresden* down to her lair off the Chilean coast, where, without coal or friends, she was hammered by shellfire and then blew herself up.

The albatrosses also did great execution among those of the *Gneisenau* who had survived the shell holocaust of December 8th. They had wings of three to four yards span, and they 'surveyed the field of the dead and avidly sought prey. It was just as well to have a spar in the hand to defend oneself. One of our young officers, noticing a bird swooping down on a man, shouted to the latter: "Hit him on the paws".' In spite of the albatrosses, the devastated condition of the cruiser before she went down, the difficulties of rescue from the cold, choppy sea, there were more survivors from the *Gneisenau* than all the other ships together. The *Invincible* collected 108, the *Inflexible* sixty-two, and the *Carnarvon*, in spite of the tragedy with the whaler, dragged twenty live men on board before darkness brought an end to rescue operations. It fell to the *Inflexible* to house the élite, including Commander Pochhammer, the senior survivor, and six other officers. Every care and comfort was given to the defeated. First they were stripped and massaged to ease the savage cramp which soon seized all those dragged from the water. Dressed in thick woollen underclothes, they sipped brandy and hot soup, and were laid in bunks wherever these could be made available. After experiencing the usual over-excited garrulousness which normally accompanies shock, 'most of them could not sleep that night', an officer of the *Inflexible* reported, 'the scenes in their ship were so terrible. To see one's best friend torn to bits, or rush on

deck one huge wound covered with blood and just have time to send
his love home, is terrible.'

Commander Pochhammer was treated with special care and
deference, and found himself that evening tucked up in the *Inflexible*'s vacant admiral's cabin, complete with hot water bottle, a
bottle of wine and a jug of warm water. There he was told of the
death of Captain Maerker, and was promised the names of all those
who had been rescued so that their relatives could be informed: for
now the post of C-in-C of the decimated East Asiatic Squadron had
fallen on this officer. He was not allowed to rest for long. 'I was
hardly installed in my new cabin,' he wrote later, 'when the commander's steward appeared and announced that dinner was served.
in the officer's mess. . . . My covering was not exactly princely . . .
being a travelling rug which I had wrapped around my still stiff
limbs. I then raised myself, and, assisted by two men, passed the
sentry in front of the cabin, who saluted me, and reached without
mishap the table.' The tablecloth struck Pochhammer as an unusual
luxury, even if it was stained with coal dust from the interrupted
early morning coaling. It was a 'scratch' meal, just ham and eggs,
and with it—'what do you like, sherry or port?' He shared the table
with the battle cruiser's officers: a genial crowd, he found them,
'and if all Englishmen were like those in the *Inflexible* we should be
able to get on with them'. One by one the other surviving unwounded
officers joined Pochhammer, six of them in all, a pathetic fragment
of those who had lived and worked together for so long in the
Gneisenau. From the first officer there was just 'a silent greeting, a
momentary gleam in the eyes' of recognition; 'and expressions of
delight at seeing each other alive again'.

Later that evening, while recovering on one of the wardroom's
leather sofas, Pochhammer was handed a telegram from Admiral
Sturdee. 'Please convey to Commander of *Gneisenau* the C-in-C is
very gratified that your life has been spared and we all feel that the
Gneisenau fought in a most plucky manner to the end,' ran Sturdee's
message. 'We much admire the good Gunnery of both ships, we
sympathize with you in the loss of your Admiral and many officers
and men. Unfortunately, the two countries are at War, the officers
of both Navies who can count friends in the other have to carry out
their country's duty, which your Admiral and Officers worthily
maintained to the end.'

Relations between the British and their German prisoners in the

Inflexible remained genial and familiar during the brief, abortive hunt for the escaped *Dresden* and the return voyage to the Falkland Islands. There, according to Pochhammer, they terminated on an unhappy note. He was invited on board the *Invincible* for dinner with Sturdee before being sent back with the other survivors to prisoner-of-war camps in Britain. Pochhammer, still in makeshift clothes, was received by Sturdee in his day cabin. There he saw a souvenir of the battle, and confirmation of his old ship's superb shooting to the very end. It was one of the last 8·2-inch shells fired by the *Gneisenau* before she went down, and had now been carefully polished. Sturdee explained apologetically that it was this shell which had destroyed a clothing store, and had thus deprived him of the opportunity to rig out more suitably the surviving German officers. Although only a solid steel practice shell, like the shell from the *Canopus* which had struck the first blow on the *Gneisenau*, it had penetrated deep into the ship, after amputating the muzzle of one of the *Invincible*'s 4-inch secondary guns. There had been more than twenty other hits on the battle cruiser, but not a man had been killed. During the dinner with the admiral's staff and other senior officers, Sturdee questioned the German commander closely on how they had accomplished their long odyssey across the Pacific, how they had obtained coal and shipped it into their bunkers, how they had evaded Admiral Jerram and Admiral Patey and the Japanese. The German account was listened to like the revelation in the final scene of a mystery play. Sturdee wanted to know, too, about the effect of the British 12-inch-fire on the German ships. Pochhammer was not giving away any useful technical information, however, and he remained evasive yet courteous. At the end of the meal the port went round in the traditional manner, and Sturdee gave the royal toast. 'What will the admiral do?' Pochhammer asked himself anxiously. It was a difficult situation, and according to Pochhammer's memory, the British admiral was unable to meet it with appropriate tact. Sturdee had raised his glass, and his guests were watching him. 'Now you will not expect that we drink the health of the Kaiser, so . . .' the admiral began. There was a pause. 'So let us drink the health of King George.'

Pochhammer said he 'was prepared for anything but that. It was some moments before I quite grasped the meaning of the words, the outrageousness of this toast. My glass almost shivered in my hand, so angry did I feel. For a moment I meditated throwing the contents in the face of this high personage. Eventually, I controlled myself, placed my glass on the table without touching it to my lips, and left no doubt about the unpleasant impression which this gross want of tact had left upon me.'

Of the three contestants in the hunting of the East Asiatic Fleet, two had died with all their officers and men. The reputations of these admirals had been secured for all time. Von Spee had conducted his escape across the Pacific skilfully, had proved his tactical flair at Coronel, had demonstrated humility and compassion afterwards. Even his decision to attack the Falkland Islands had revealed only a minor tactical failing: it was the German intelligence services which had really led him into the trap. In his final combat he had revealed cunning and tenacity; his end was honourable and splendid. Admiral Sir Christopher Cradock's place in history is equally safe. After the breath of criticism from those who had sent him to his grave had faded, the words of a new British First Lord of the Admiralty, spoken two years later at the unveiling of his memorial, endured for all time: 'His body is separated from us by half the world, and he and his gallant comrades lie far from the pleasant homes of England. Yet they have their reward, and we are surely right in saying that theirs is an immortal place in the great role of naval heroes.'

Both these old friends who faced one another and died fighting against hopeless odds were mourned with reverence and in the certain knowledge that they had done their best. Of the admiral who wreaked vengeance and won and survived, there remained doubts among some people which lasted for the remainder of his life.

Admiral Sturdee had accomplished, quicker than anyone thought possible, almost all that had been asked of him. As he sharply countered subsequent Admiralty criticism, 'Their Lordships selected me as Commander-in-Chief to destroy the two hostile armoured cruisers and I endeavoured to the best of my ability to carry out these orders.' Four out of the total force of von Spee's five cruisers had been accounted for, the enemy admiral himself, the captains of his ships, and some 2,200 officers and men had died. It was a worse blow to Germany by far than the defeat at Coronel had been to the British. The seas had been cleared of almost every threat by surface craft to Britain's trade. Most of the numerous warships which had been scattered about the world in preparation for the sudden appearance of von Spee, could now be withdrawn and sent to reinforce Admiral Jellicoe, who was still worrying away about the quantity as well as the quality of German Dreadnoughts compared with his own. Surely here was cause for national jubilation and thanksgiving! And there was plenty of both. It was England's greatest victory at sea since the beginning of the war, and when the newspapers announcing it appeared on the streets, there were scenes of wild excitement. Now that 'Jacky' Fisher was back in the Admiralty, this was the kind of news they could expect from the navy. Poor Cradock and his men had been avenged, in no mean manner. Sturdee became a national hero overnight. At Port Stanley on Sturdee's return, Sir William Allardyce invited all the leading citizens and his defence volunteers to Government House for a drink to celebrate their release from the danger of attack, and toasts were drunk to King George and to the Royal Navy.

But it remains a sad irony that Britain's one decisive victory at sea in the First World War was clouded by doubts and soiled by personal acrimony. The man who had avenged 'Kit' Cradock received congratulatory telegrams from all over the world—from Jellicoe and Beatty and other senior admirals of the Grand Fleet, from the French and Russian admiralties, from his old friend Lord Charles Beresford, from King George himself, who signalled 'I heartily congratulate you and your officers and men on your most opportune victory.' From Lord Fisher, Sturdee received no message. This negative response was only the beginning of Sturdee's troubles. Fisher cherished to the end of his life his delight that his much-criticized battle cruisers had justified his highest hopes. On the manner of the victory's accomplishment, he retained the gravest doubts. As early as December 10th and before Sturdee's full report had been received, Fisher was writing to Churchill: ' . . . let us be self-restrained—*not too exultant!—till we know details! Perhaps their guns never reached us!* . . . it may have been like shooting pheasants: the pheasants not shooting back! Not too much glory for us, only great satisfaction. . . .' When Fisher later received details and heard that Sturdee had allowed the *Dresden* to escape (not a total annihilation after all!), he was furious, and subjected his subordinate and old opponent to a series of blistering enquiries. 'Report fully reason for the course which you have followed since the action . . .' he demanded, and proposed bringing back the battle cruisers without their admiral. Sturdee, he insisted, should not be allowed home until he had completed his task, and this he must accomplish in an armoured cruiser. It was a stinging insult. To Jellicoe he wrote, 'Sturdee's criminal ineptitude in not sending a vessel to Punta Arenas at the close of the action on December 8th to cable result to Admiralty and to get information from the British Consul there (who held the cable!) has disastrously kept from you light cruisers now hunting *Dresden*. . . .' Fisher remained unsatisfied by Sturdee's increasingly tart explanatory replies, the last of which ended, 'I submit that my being called upon in three separate telegrams to give reasons for my subsequent action was unexpected.' Fisher told him this language was improper. 'Such observations must not be repeated,' he told the C-in-C.

Winston Churchill used all his tact to diminish the passions between his First Sea Lord and the victorious admiral. First he persuaded Fisher that to leave Sturdee in the South Seas with an old armoured cruiser was 'scarcely suited to his rank and standing, and woefully out of harmony with his recent achievement'. Fisher, though 'much vexed', yielded. Sturdee was therefore ordered home, Fisher viewed with dismay the inevitable hero's welcome in London. The man did not deserve it. The record, in Fisher's eyes, did not justify the cheers of the populace. First, Sturdee had 'wanted to delay his departure from Plymouth, and had he done so, the Germans would have swallowed the *Canopus*' and gone on to commit further depredations off the African coast. Then his tactics in the battle were 'dilatory and theatrical'; Fisher compared them with the over-extravagant style of the English actor William Terriss. He had been slow before, during and after the action, thus allowing the *Dresden* to get away scotfree. It was only at the persuasion of others that he had reached the Falkland Islands in time.

When Sturdee arrived in London to be fêted, Fisher tried to hustle him away at once to his new command with the Grand Fleet. Sturdee refused. He had been summoned to Buckingham Palace to give King George and Queen Mary personally an account of his victory. But he was away again in forty-eight hours, several of which were occupied in waiting in the Admiralty to be received, with extreme reluctance, by Fisher. Fisher gave him five minutes, asked him nothing about the battle and castigated him for his failure to catch the *Dresden*. In case Sturdee still nursed any dreams that he had, in fact, brought about a marvellous victory, Fisher greatly reduced his list of officers and men recommended for honours; and doctored his official report on the battle in order to deny him some of the credit he claimed for himself and his squadron.

Admiral Lord Fisher had for long been noted, and feared, for his personal and unremitting attacks on those who opposed him and thus, by his reckoning, brought discredit to his beloved Royal Navy. He believed Sturdee to be insubordinate, and a fool. But if Fisher had been Sturdee's only detractor, the passions in the service would not have become so inflamed, nor would his reputation and his victorious fight have been discredited among so many. To many knowledgable people inside and outside the navy who studied the course of the battle and its aftermath with care, Sturdee's handling of the situation had been clumsy and inept. But for the overwhelming forces at his command, and the remarkable good fortune with the weather, von Spee might well have escaped. Churchill himself, while deploring Fisher's extreme words and actions, shared his misgivings about Sturdee's tactics. Like Fisher, he did not send the private letter of congratulation circumstances normally demanded. Churchill was also present at that tense five-minute meeting with Sturdee at the Admiralty, at which, according to the infuriated Sturdee, 'neither evinced the slightest interest in the engagement'. One of Sturdee's critics wrote to Fisher, 'No one in history was ever kicked on to a pedestal of fame like Sturdee. If he had been allowed to pack all the shirts he wanted to take . . . Sturdee would have been looking for von Spee still!' Other students of the battle uncharitably pointed out that while von Spee had destroyed the *Good Hope* and *Monmouth* in little more than an hour under appalling conditions, with an expenditure of 160,000 pounds of heavy shell, Sturdee with much faster and more powerful ships had spent the whole of a clear day to send the *Gneisenau* and *Scharnhorst* to the bottom, and had used up a million pounds of shell, almost emptying his magazines.

Those who had been at the receiving end confirmed the 'really feeble' results of Sturdee's 12-inch gunfire. 'It was not surprising that our ship had not been able in the long run to resist guns of such heavy calibre,' wrote the *Gneisenau*'s First Officer, 'but the time they had taken to destroy us had been excessive.' Captain Herbert W. Richmond, one of the keenest brains in the Admiralty, who had vainly persuaded Sturdee when he was still Chief of Staff to send out battle cruisers to hunt von Spee, stingingly summed up the intellectuals' view in his diary by describing it as 'an irony that

Sturdee, the man who more than anyone else is responsible for the loss of Cradock's squadron, should be the person who profits principally from it, and should be made a national hero! . . . the enemy come in sight . . . running into his arms and saving him the trouble of searching for them. He puts to sea with his squadron of greatly superior force . . . and has only to steer after them and sink them, which he not unnaturally does. If he didn't, he would indeed be a duffer. Yet for this simple piece of service he is acclaimed as a marvellous strategist and tactician! So are reputations made!'

These were no times for public dispute and recrimination and indulgence in the British habit of self-denigration. A victory was too priceless an asset in the dark days for British arms at the end of 1914. To the general public, Doveton Sturdee's reputation was indeed secure. Apart from some mild criticism in *The Times*, no breath of scandal was allowed to diminish the strength of the accolades for Sturdee and his men. He was awarded a Baronetcy by King George, received the thanks of Parliament and a grant of £10,000, and after Fisher's death was given the ultimate promotion, to the rank of Admiral of the Fleet. Sir Doveton Sturdee, Bart, spent his last years restoring to her original condition the old wooden battleship *Victory*, in which Admiral Lord Nelson had secured for Britain her last decisive sea triumph at Trafalgar just 130 years before Sturdee's death in 1935.

With the destruction by Captain John Luce of the fugitive *Dresden* off Robinson Crusoe's island on March 14, 1915, the British Navy accounted for the last of Germany's raiding cruisers. It had taken seven months and ten days to round them all up and relieve British trade of the anxieties which had beset every merchantman in the Atlantic, Pacific and Indian oceans since the beginning of the war. Of the East Asiatic Squadron's officers and men, almost all had been killed or drowned. Not one of the German cruisers on the high seas at the beginning of the war got back through the British blockade to Germany. Only one small and pathetic memorial to the holocaust off the Falklands is said to have made the journey safely. More than a year later, fishermen off the Schleswig coast of Germany sighted 'a little water-worn dinghy', twelve feet long. After some eighteen months of war, the North Sea was then thick with pathetic drifting flotsam and wreckage of ships of all kinds sunk by torpedo, mine or gunfire. This little boat had come farther than most, for on it was inscribed just decipherably the name *Nürnberg*. Its instinctive navigation over 7,000 miles had been faultless, for the German naval base at Cuxhaven was only a few miles distant. It was the only memorial that the Countess von Spee could claim of her son Otto, and the last battle of her husband and her younger son Heinrich. 'It may be,' wrote an officer who did survive, 'that in her dim blind way this fragment of a once-fine cruiser, all that was left of a splendid squadron, was inspired to bring to her far-away northern home the news of a year-old tragedy.'

Appendix

Rear-Admiral H. E. Dannreuther, DSO, recently discovered the lost report he wrote immediately after the Battle of the Falkland Islands and which he had not seen for more than fifty years. It is of an informal nature and of special value because it remains uncoloured by the influences and prejudices of the passing years which have reduced the authenticity of so many later accounts of the engagement. In addition, Lieutenant Dannreuter, Gunnery Officer of HMS *Invincible*, and stationed in the foretop of the flagship throughout the battle, was in a unique position to observe both the English and German gunnery. The following are extracts from this report. (Admiral Dannreuter was stationed in the same position in the *Invincible* at the Battle of Jutland eighteen months later when the ship was blown up by German shellfire. He was thrown into the sea, to become the senior of only six survivors of a complement of 1,032.)

The fight was down wind and the dense columns of smoke we were making made gunlaying very difficult from the two after turrets— at the same time a large proportion of the ship was hidden from the enemy. The position was a bad one from our point of view but might have been a positive advantage if the Director Installation had been completed.

The ranges were much longer than we had dreamt of. Our maximum range at the time was 16,000 yards with the guns at extreme elevation. We intended to fight at 12,000 yards so as to be at a range compatible, we hoped, with good practice and at 12,000 yards our 6-inch side armour was likely to keep out the German 8·2 A.P. (armour-piercing) shell . . . the enemy turned to port and opened fire: much to our surprise they straddled us with their third salvo at 15,500 yards. . . .

The firing of both German ships was very good, salvoes were fired well together and the spread appeared to be small. But I cannot guarantee about the spread as I could only see the shorts, and splashes in line always appear closer together than they really are. Their fire discipline must have been excellent—they went on firing consistent and well-aimed salvoes till they started to list heavily and go down. The *Gneisenau*'s officers stated that the ship was in a terrible state before she sank. Her decks were red hot in places and the ship was burning everywhere; great holes had been torn in the decks and from the level of the bridge most of the main deck could be seen. . . .

The *Inflexible* was hit three times and suffered no damage except that the head of her Main Derrick was broken off. The *Invincible* was hit 22 times by 8·2-inch and 5·9-inch, mostly 8·2-inch, and suffered a good deal of damage, though fortunately the fighting equipment remained practically intact. Curiously enough the three 8·2-inch shells that did most damage did not burst. One struck the armour forward and on the water line and flooded the two bow compartments. Another entered the side 10 feet below the water line below 'P' turret and just below the side armour. This shell made a large hole and broke up against the internal armour round 'P' handling room. The bunker was flooded and gave the ship a bit of a list. However, we came all the way back to Gibraltar with these compartments flooded.

The third shell hit No 2 4-inch gun starboard, broke it in half and wrecked the mounting, then descended at a slope of 48 degrees through three decks and squashed all the 3-inch voice pipes from the Fore Top to the fore T.S. We have this shell still on board. The Wardroom, Canteen and Sick Bay were entirely wrecked. Much water from damaged fire mains found its way into the store-rooms and bunkers. The decks above the bunkers and store-rooms were badly pierced and in many places the water simply ran down into these store-rooms and ruined some valuable stores.

The incendiary effect of German shell was very small. Only one fire occurred and that was in the Sick Bay where some bedding caught alight and burned fiercely till it was put out by the Fire Brigade. . . .

The 8·2-inch shell which burst in the wardroom completely wrecked every item of furniture, smashing the table, sideboard and chairs into small fragments, bulging up the deck overhead and blowing a hole 6 foot square in the deck beneath, but no signs of fire or even of the paintwork being scorched. Several shells hit the upper deck and then went through the ship's side—the angle of descent being in one or two cases as much as 60 degrees.

Primary Control from Fore Top was used throughout. At times the control was very difficult as we were firing down wind the whole time and the view from aloft was much interfered with by gun smoke and funnel smoke.

Range Finders were of little use and any form of range-finder plotting was impossible owing to the difficulty of observation and high range. In fact as far as this particular action was concerned it would have made no difference if the ship had not had a single Range Finder or Dumaresq or any plotting outfit on board.

During the latter part of the action with the *Gneisenau* [she] continually zig-zagged to try and avoid being hit, altering course every few minutes about two points either side of her normal course. This alteration of course could not be detected by Range Finder or by eye and continual spotting corrections were necessary. The rate being fairly high and changing every few minutes from opening to closing I found the only effective means was to keep the rate at zero and continually spot on the target. By this means we managed to hit her now and again.

An assistant spotter with a telescope at the fore end of the top was very useful, for by a system of dual observation we were able to dodge the splashes of enemy's shorts which sometimes entirely blocked the view of one or other of the spotters but rarely of both at the same time. I found ordinary prism binoculars best. With them I could move about freely and stand upright.

Resting glasses, etc., on the edge of the top was not practicable owing to the jar. The top also shook very violently especially when 'A' turret fired. This was caused principally by the starboard strut having been shot through.

The service stereoscopes were of no use for it was quite impossible to keep them steady enough for effective spotting either when slung from the canopy or held in the hands.

'Overs' were rarely seen for they were hidden by the enemy's gun and funnel smoke.

'Hits' were often very difficult to see. We usually detected them by seeing a flash and if the flash was not followed by a small cloud of brown smoke we knew it was a hit and that the flash was not from one of the enemy's guns. I fancy, but cannot vouch for it, that a good many of our Common Shell did not explode when hitting the water or hitting the ship.

The enemy altered course 16 points on several occasions. This caused some of the gunlayers to mistake the stern for the bow. The bow wash of the enemy was hardly visible and masts and funnels were perfectly upright. This error was corrected by verbal order to aim at right- or left-hand end of the ship.

. . . The conditions of laying from 'P', 'Q' and 'X' turrets were at times extremely difficult owing to our smoke; the gunlayers having to fire at the flashes of the enemy's guns. . . .

The blast from the 8·2-inch shell that burst inside the starboard strut blew open the manhole door leading to the control top. The blast was somewhat severe and knocked everyone down in the top, tore the heavy Mk VI Dumaresq from its moorings and wrecked the rate transmitter. It did not do much material harm but to be knocked down is disconcerting to the control officer and entails missing the fall of a salvo. . . .

On the way up to Montevideo every effort was made in the ship to remove all traces of the action. The ship was painted overall and the holes in the deck and superstructure were either plated over, or covered with canvas and cortisene. This proved to be a wise precaution as at Montevideo some influential Argentine gentlemen with a letter of introduction from the British Minister of Buenos Aires visited the ship and were shown round the upper deck. They were much impressed by the fact that we had suffered no damage in the action. I understand that this incident, small though it was, did much to enhance our naval prestige in Buenos Aires, which had been much shaken by the disaster at Coronel. . . .

We arrived at Montevideo on December 20th and remained there for the day. Our principal reason for calling there was to confirm some of the wireless signals that had been made to us from Ceritos. Ceritos wireless station is close to Montevideo and besides being the only means of communication with the Falkland Islands was also our only means of communication with the Admiralty and a number of signals made required confirmation.

Our wireless officer visited the station and reported that from the numerous wireless signals made from Ceritos there was strong evidence to show that the German Battle Cruisers *Seydlitz*, *Moltke* and *von der Tann* were within wireless touch of Montevideo. We had heard continual rumours of these ships being in the Atlantic, especially the *von der Tann*. Our situation was not an easy one. We were by ourselves in a somewhat damaged condition with very little ammunition on board and were hardly a match for three German Battle Cruisers. A cable was sent to the Admiralty asking for news of these German ships and reporting that until we received more definite information we were proceeding south again to the Falkland Islands to concentrate there with the *Inflexible* and *Australia*. We received a reply from the Admiralty ten hours later to say that these ships had a few days previously been seen in the North Sea. So we turned north again.

The origin of these persistent rumours was probably as follows. [On the way out] we boarded as many steamers as possible and it was very noticeable how nearly every ship whether English or foreign endeavoured to escape, firmly believing, till the boarding officer arrived on board, that we were German battle cruisers— probably the merchant ships were deceived by the light colour of our paint, which was like the German colour and much lighter than the colour they had been accustomed to see in English men-of-war. The result of this was that a German battle cruiser was reported to be in the West Indies. She was reported to be the *von der Tann*, but was really the *Princess Royal*. Later on two more German battle cruisers were reported to be in the Atlantic as well and were said to be the *Moltke* and *Seydlitz* but were really the *Invincible* and *Inflexible*. These rumours, once started, were spread as much as possible by the large number of wireless stations in South America that were heavily subsidized and practically run by Germans with a view probably of frightening our trade. The call signs of these three ships were often made and we got them on one or two occasions. So it turned out we were hunting our own shadows. . . .

Select Bibliography

GEOFFREY BENNETT: *Coronel and Falklands* (London, 1965)
WINSTON S. CHURCHILL: *The World Crisis, 1911–14* (Vol 1) (London, 1923)
JULIAN S. CORBETT: *Naval Operations* (Vol 1) (London, 1920)
CHRISTOPHER CRADOCK: *Whispers from the Fleet* (Portsmouth, 1907)
C. DICK: *Das Kreuzergeschwader* (Berlin, 1917)
R. H. GIBSON: *Three Years of Naval Warfare* (London, 1919)
P. GIORDANI: *The German Colonial Empire* (London, 1916)
HAROLD HICKLING: *Sailor at Sea* (London, 1965)
LLOYD HIRST: *Coronel and After* (London, 1934)
EDWIN P. HOYT: *The Last Cruise of the* Emden (New York and London, 1966)
JOHN IRVING: *Coronel and the Falklands* (London, 1927)
H. KIRCHOFF: *Maximilian Graf von Spee* (Leipzig, 1915)
HERMANN LOREY: *Der Krieg zur See, 1914–18. Das Kreuzeschwader* (Berlin, 1922)
L. MAHN: *Fürst Bismarck. Sein Politisches Leben und Wirken* (Vol 5) (Berlin, 1891)
ARTHUR J. MARDER: *Portrait of an Admiral: The Life and Papers of Admiral Sir Herbert Richmond* (London, 1952)
ARTHUR J. MARDER: *From the Dreadnought to Scapa Flow* (Vol II) (London, 1965)
ARTHUR J. MARDER, Editor: *Fear God and Dread Nought, the correspondence of Admiral of the Fleet Lord Fisher of Kilverstone* (Vol III) (London, 1959)
K. MIDDLEMASS: *Command of the Far Seas* (London, 1961)
E. MILLINGTON-DRAKE: *The Drama of Graf von Spee and the Battle of the River Plate* (London, 1964)
BARRIE PITT: *Coronel and Falkland* (London, 1960)
HANS POCHHAMMER: *Before Jutland, Admiral von Spee's Last Voyage* (London, 1931)
S. ROUTLEDGE: *The Mystery of Easter Island* (London, 1919)
H. SPENCER-COOPER: *The Battle of the Falkland Islands* (London, 1919)
A. J. P. TAYLOR: *Germany's First Bid for Colonies, 1884–5* (London, 1938)
M. E. TOWNSEND: *The Rise and Fall of Germany's Colonial Empire, 1884–1918* (New York, 1930)
R. VERNER: *The Battle Cruisers at the Action of the Falkland Islands* (London, 1920)
R. WILSON: *The First Year of the Great War* (London, 1915)

The Cornhill Magazine, 1917; Naval Staff Monographs; K. G. B. Dewar: 'The Coronel Campaign'; *Brassey's Naval Annual; The Pacific Commercial Advertiser; The Honolulu Star Bulletin; The Times*, London; Dannreuther Papers.

Index

Index

Index